4/16/11

To Shirley —
God bless and enjoy!

Kathi Macias

The

TRAIN-OF-THOUGHT

WRITING METHOD:

Practical, User-Friendly Help for Beginning Writers

by

Kathi Macias

authorHOUSE™

1663 LIBERTY DRIVE, SUITE 200
BLOOMINGTON, INDIANA 47403
(800) 839-8640
WWW.AUTHORHOUSE.COM

First published by AuthorHouse 6/11/07

ISBN: 1-4208-3259-X (sc)

Library of Congress Control Number: 2005901100

Printed in the United States of America
Bloomington, Indiana

This book is printed on acid-free paper.

ENDORSEMENTS

Do you have a dream of becoming a writer? Would you like to learn the ins and outs of marketing your manuscripts? Have you already been rejected by editor after editor and want to find out what you might be doing wrong? If your answer is "yes," then this is the book for you. Kathi Macias is one terrific teacher!

—Martha Bolton, former staff writer for Bob Hope and author of over fifty books of humor, including *Cooking with Hot Flashes*

Train-of-Thought is a terrific resource for unpublished writers. This book will get you on track with your book project. Highly recommended!

—Randy Ingermanson, author of Christy award winning novels *Transgression* and *Oxygen*

The writer's maxim "show, don't tell" is what Kathi Macias helps novice writers discover and experienced writers remember. *The Train-of-Thought Writing Method* brims with first-class examples, simple exercises, and basic instruction from a pro to help jumpstart your writing.

—Don S. Otis, author and president of Creative Resources, Inc.

I'd heard of the train concept in the past and have used it myself but not with the depth, clarity, and practicality that Kathi Macias has developed in her book. I'm very impressed with her concept and know it will be popular with beginning writers. I would be glad to recommend it when I teach about writing.

—Kathy Collard Miller, speaker and author of forty-seven books including *Princess to Princess* (Cook)

This one's right on track! Kathi Macias has taken one of my favorite teaching methods—the train of thought—and put it into an educational and entertaining text that will become a standard for teaching beginning writers how to write publishable material. I can wholeheartedly endorse this book with its straightforward and engaging writing style.

—Sally E. Stuart, *Christian Writers' Market Guide*

Finally, a usable workbook on the train-of-thought formula! This will be a big help to writers in nailing the all-important focus and format for publishable articles and books. Kathi has put her years of experience into a valuable tool for aspiring writers.

—Elaine Wright Colvin, founder/director of Writers Information Network (WIN)

I am so glad to see that Kathi Macias, with her many years of writing, editing, and teaching experience, has committed this excellent writing method to book form. It is long overdue, and will be a real plus for new writers trying to break into the competitive world of publishing. I highly recommend it!

—Susan Titus Osborn, author of twenty-eight books and director of the Christian Communicator Manuscript Critique service

Kathi Macias takes the complex and often confusing process of writing for publication and breaks it down into simple steps that are easy for the beginning or aspiring writer to understand and apply. The train analogy makes the concepts clear and fun to learn. The examples she uses, which are based on best-selling novels, classics, and Kathi's own publications, provide a wide range of applications that readers can study and analyze as they seek to create their own attention-grabbing writing. All aboard!

—Kathy Ide, author, editor, and founder of The Christian PEN (Proofreaders and Editors Network)

The Train-of-Thought Writing Method by Kathi Macias is fresh, friendly, and good for an occasional chuckle. It offers genuine help for the beginning and/or unpublished writer, and I am pleased to recommend it in my workshops and seminars.

—Laurel West, journalist, speaker/teacher, and author of *Beloved Dissident*

DEDICATION

To all those who share my love for words: May you be blessed by the One who has called us to "write the vision…and make it plain."

To my husband, Al: Thank you for being my partner on this great journey…and the next.

To my sons, Al, Mike, and Chris: May you always walk with the One who loves you even more than I.

To my mother, who one day soon will "depart from Narnia" and go on ahead of us to join my father, as together they begin the first chapter of the Great Story that no one on earth has ever read….

ACKNOWLEDGMENTS

Thanks to all those who over the years have taught the train-of-thought writing method, especially the late Georgiana Walker, who first introduced me to this great system.

Thanks, too, to all those who encouraged me to pursue this endeavor and/or kept me on task throughout the process: first and foremost, Laurel West, whose "polishing" techniques made this manuscript shine; also, Chip MacGregor, Nikki Arana, Jane Hall, Martha Bolton, Randy Ingermanson, Don Otis, Kathy Collard Miller, Sally Stuart, Elaine Wright Colvin, Susan Titus Osborn, and Kathy Ide.

CONTENTS

INTRODUCTION

As the author of fifteen books and countless articles and short stories, I am constantly asked the same question: Where do you get your ideas?

For someone with as active an imagination as mine, ideas are not the problem. I have more ideas than time to utilize them! The real question is: How do you effectively take those ideas and convert them to saleable manuscripts? And that's what this book is all about.

It is said that writing is 10 percent inspiration and 90 percent perspiration. I absolutely agree, and I'm sure most successful writers would echo my sentiments: Inspiration—or coming up with ideas—is the easy part. But I contend that writing itself is not an easy profession, though I've heard it argued that writing is indeed easy, so long as you're willing to sit down at the typewriter/computer/word processor and open a vein. Ouch! There's a lot of truth in that statement of absolute commitment, as you will see as we work our way through this book.

Over the years I have spoken with and taught beginning writers from all around the world, in all sorts of settings. I have helped them review, edit, and rewrite their work, and I have found one common thread among those would-be writers who eventually become published authors: They are willing to devote themselves to the not-so-fun, open-the-vein part of writing—the 90 percent perspiration.

Most all writers enter the industry with some serious misconceptions. I know I imagined myself spending at least as much time on book-signing tours as sitting in front of the computer trying to get my thoughts on paper. But here it is, nearly twenty years later, and I'm still spending a minimum of 90 percent of my professional time sitting in front of the computer, writing and rewriting—and rewriting again.

Because when it comes down to it that's what successful writing is really all about—the rewriting. I once heard someone say that good books are not written, they are rewritten. How true that is—and how difficult and discouraging it can be at times. But through the years I have found what I consider to be the simplest and most practical writing method available—the train-of-thought method (though it may be known by other names as well). I wish I could tell you that this wonderful writing method originated with me, or at least that I knew where it actually did originate. But it didn't, and I don't, though I diligently tried to trace it back to its origin. I do know that others, including the late Georgiana Walker, have taught the method at writers' conferences for years. I also know that author Omer Henry mentioned it in a chapter of his book titled *Writing and Selling Magazine Articles*, first published by The Writer, Inc., in 1962. Beyond that I have been unable to locate any information or printed material on the subject.

And so I have decided to put it in writing myself. This is not a book about proper grammar or punctuation, or how best to choose the voice or set the scene for your great American novel. There are already countless books covering those subjects, if that's what you're looking for. But if you want to know how best to take your thoughts and dreams and put them into a clear, compelling, readable manuscript, then this is the book for you. Having personally seen the train-of-thought writing method help so many new writers learn to organize, write, and polish their ideas into successful manuscripts, I offer this book to those who would do the same. May it direct and encourage you as you enter into the 90 percent perspiration phase of your writing career—the serious phase through which true writers are formed.

Chapter One

"Laying the Track"

Have you ever made the mistake of asking an eight-year-old what a movie was about? I have—and the results were brutal. Nearly an hour later, as he finally wrapped up his nonstop, blow-by-blow report with "And that's what it was about," my eyes were glazed over and I was bordering on comatose. All I could think of was, *I just asked what time it was; I didn't want to know how to make the clock!* Honestly, a simple "It was a story about a dog named Snickers" would have sufficed.

Eight-year-olds, however, have not yet learned to focus. Their attention span is still somewhat akin to that of a housefly, so I knew it was pointless to try to explain to him that I simply wanted a one-line synopsis of the movie. Better to cut my losses and make a run for it before he started telling me about the sequel.

But are adults that much different? To be more specific, are writers that much different? We should be. In fact, we *must* be if we are to be effective communicators. But are we?

One of the most frequent problems I see among new writers is a desire to "eat the entire elephant." I'm sure you've heard the saying that the only way to eat an elephant is one bite at a time, and that's a great way to approach writing. For instance, if you want to write a story about your family vacation to the Redwoods, you need to stick to what actually happened on that trip. You should, of course, include enough information about your family, the scenery, the weather, and the magnificent trees to bring your story to life, but you don't have to write an encyclopedia on trees in general. Or, if you are thinking of writing about a particular spiritual experience you once had, you don't want to attempt to write an apologetic on the entire Bible. In other words, successful writing is about finding and keeping your focus, unlike the eight-year-old with the limited attention span who rambled on and on about the movie because he wasn't able to formulate and express one clear thought. In essence, he was trying to eat the entire elephant in one big bite. I've seen a lot of writers attempt the same thing, and it simply does not work.

Now because you are reading this book I assume you are a writer—a beginning writer and/or an as-yet unpublished writer, possibly, but a writer nonetheless. Therefore I will also assume that you have at least one great idea burning in your chest, crying to get out and make its way into a book or a magazine. If I were to ask you, as I wanted to ask that eight-year-old, for a one-line synopsis of your masterpiece, would you be able to give it to me? If not, then I have to ask you another question: Do you really know what your idea is about?

Think about it for a moment. If you can't summarize your would-be manuscript (or maybe one you've already written) in one line, that tells me you aren't really clear on the theme or purpose of the piece. How then can you expect your readers to figure it out? After all, our readers are the key to the success of anything we write. My journalism professor at USC once told me, "Our job as writers is not so much to express ourselves as it is to effectively communicate an idea to our readers." If someone reads one of my books and comes away scratching his head and mumbling, "I wonder what that was all about," he's certainly not going to read my next book or recommend my work to anyone else. And that, in the extremely competitive publishing world, can be fatal to any writing career.

It's not that we don't want to make our readers think. All writers have some sort of underlying message that we want readers to chew on for a while, hopefully even after they've finished reading our work. But we also want them to be clear on what that message is. The only way to assure that happening is first to be sure that we ourselves are clear on what we are trying to say.

Every well constructed object, whether a twenty-five-story building or a brief magazine article, must begin with a firm foundation. And that's what this first chapter is about: properly laying the foundation—or in this case, the "track"—of your manuscript. We begin at the beginning, and if we work through the entire piece correctly, then when we're finished we will have come full circle, ending up right back where we started, standing upon the firm foundation that supports the entire manuscript and leaves our readers with a clear and satisfying takeaway thought.

And so I challenge you: Can you capture the heart of that masterpiece that is burning inside of you and write it down in one brief, succinct statement or synopsis, understanding that this statement is the "takeaway" you want to impart to your readers? In other words, when your readers finish reading your piece, will they have been able to find the meaning of your manuscript within the one-line synopsis that was the starting place for your writing?

Before we begin trying to isolate and write down that one-line statement for your masterpiece, let's take a look at a couple of brief writings that I've dug out and dusted off from my own ancient files. The first is one of the very short "about town" columns that I wrote for the local newspaper way back in the mid-'80s. The weekly column was called "My Two Cents' Worth" because that's just about how much they paid me to write it, and also because that's all it was—my two cents' worth of opinion. So trust me when I tell you that the piece you are about to read is not very deep.

As you read through this column, listen for its heartbeat, its theme, its purpose, and then, in the space following, write a one-sentence statement of what you believe that theme to be.

***

You know, people often kid about California becoming so populated that it will one day sink right into the Pacific Ocean. Well, if that ever happens, it will all be because of New Year's Day.

Seriously, how many people from the Golden State, along with millions of other Americans, spend New Year's Day parked in front of their television sets watching football? I know I do. In fact, I wouldn't dream of spending it anyplace else. I love football, and besides, that's what New Year's Day is all about, right?

But we Californians have an advantage. Because we live in this beautiful, sunny piece of paradise, we can go outside at halftime without first having to put on our long johns, two sweaters, a ski suit, a parka, a scarf, and gloves. If we did we'd never get it all on, get outside, and then get back in before the second half.

And that's the problem. All across the rest of the country, while we pampered West Coasterners are enduring yet another one of our brutal California winters, other people are huddled together inside the relative safety of their homes, listening to the wind howling outside as they watch the Rose Bowl game on television. And what do they see as they sit there, shivering and sipping their hot cider? All those UCLA fans jumping up and down in their T-shirts and Bermuda shorts!

Think about it. Those poor non-Californians who have to drag themselves from their comfortable couches and brave the outdoors to bring in some more firewood, only to have their eyelashes crack and fall off from the cold, are watching all those suntanned Californians sitting in the bleachers, slurping cold drinks. How long could you take it if you were in their shoes? How long before you called a family conference and said, "Okay, gang, this is it. We're heading west."

So if any of you happen to be lucky enough to get tickets for next year's Rose Bowl game, do me a favor, will you? Bundle up real good, drink hot chocolate, and shiver a lot during the game. You never know who may be watching. And after all, it's a small price to pay to keep California afloat.

***

Okay, I warned you that it wasn't deep. But there's a reason for that—besides the lousy salary they paid me, of course. I wanted you to see that any piece—short, long, serious, humorous, fiction, nonfiction, deep or shallow—has to have a theme, a one-sentence statement that pulls it all together. With that in mind, think about what I wrote in my about-town column and then write down what you see as that one-sentence statement in the space below. (If working in a group, pair off and discuss your statements when you're through.)

_____

_____

_____

_____

_____

_____

Now let's compare statements, keeping in mind that the words don't have to be exactly the same but the thought should be similar. Here is my one-sentence statement: *California is becoming overpopulated because people in other parts of the country see our wonderful winter weather when they watch the Rose Bowl game on television.* That's what I would tell someone who asked me what my column was about, and it's what I would hope the readers would "take away" with them after finishing the piece.

All right, let's try one more, this time with the synopsis for a novel called *Shooting Star*, which I co-authored with former football great and embroidery connoisseur Rosey Grier in 1993. Your job is to condense this 562-word synopsis down to one sentence, summarizing the heart of the story, the takeaway that was left with the readers when they finished the book.

***

Brett Holiday's breath comes in short gasps and his chest heaves as he pushes himself onward, down the street, around the corner, and into the trashcan-lined alley. His shirt is plastered to his still muscular but aging body.

He wipes the sweat from his brow and wonders when it was that he first crossed that line from honored hero of the gridiron to fading-fast, backup quarterback. It was April 1989, many years since he'd first begun his professional football career. Why hadn't he seen it coming? Did he really think he could stay young forever? Did he honestly believe his faithful fans wouldn't turn fickle when a younger, stronger, more agile quarterback was introduced into the starting lineup?

The roar of yesterday's crowd echoes in his ears, blocking out the flat, slapping sounds of his well-worn Nikes hitting the pavement. It also blocks out the scraping noise of a trashcan being jerked into place. But Brett's eyes are still sharp and clear, and the flash of movement behind the can doesn't escape his attention.

Every instinct warns him to push on, to ignore whomever or whatever is hiding there. Better yet, to escape while he still has the chance. But his heart—or is it simply his curiosity?—won't let him.

That's when Brett Holiday, one-time star quarterback for the Los Angeles Rams, meets Elmore "Fox" Richards, a tall, skinny, streetwise black kid who has all the answers—but little else. Abandoned by his mother at the age of four, Fox has spent his life moving in and out of foster homes. Now, at age twelve, his chances of being adopted have all but vanished. His insolent, chip-on-the-shoulder attitude makes it difficult even to find a foster home that will take him. And so he spends his lonely days—and even lonelier nights—at a state-run shelter.

Disgusted and discouraged with the shelter and dreaming of a better life, Fox has run away. Having spent several very cold nights on the streets, he is rummaging through the trash in hopes of finding something to keep him warm—and maybe even something to eat—before night falls once again. His hiding place discovered, he now stands toe-to-toe—and almost eyeball-to-eyeball—with this fast-approaching-middle-age, sweat-soaked white man who wants to know what in the world he is doing hiding in the alley. Scared, alone, and hungry, Fox juts out his jaw defiantly and informs Brett that it's a free country and he can hang out in an alley if he wants to, and if Brett doesn't like it, what's he plan to do about it?

Brett has no idea what he plans to do about it or why he even bothered to stop and talk with this punk kid with the lousy attitude, who obviously wants no part of him. Even so, he cannot bring himself to leave. Instead, he makes a silent, almost subconscious commitment to stay—a commitment that will stretch out a lot longer than he ever could have imagined.

The developing relationship between Brett and Fox is a volatile one, full of frustration, anger, and tears. But Brett becomes more and more determined to show his new friend what love really is. In doing so, he once again finds the courage and renewed faith to wish on a shooting star, rather than hanging his worn-out dreams on a fading one.

***

Ready? Okay, give it a try. (Again, if working in a group, pair off and discuss statements when you're through.)

_____

_____

_____

_____

_____

_____

Now compare what you've written to my one-sentence statement: *An aging white football star finds new meaning and purpose in life when he befriends a homeless black kid with an attitude.* In one sentence, that's what my book was about.

How did you do? Close? Almost the same? Slightly different? It wasn't all that difficult, was it? But now a word of caution: Reading a completed piece and then coming up with the one-sentence statement that summarizes its theme is a lot easier than coming up with that statement *before* the piece is written, while it's still in the thinking or formative stage. And yet that's exactly what you need to do if you want your own writing to be smooth and cohesive and meaningful. Can you imagine climbing aboard a train and expecting a pleasant ride if the train had no track? The track has to be laid before the train can go anywhere.

And that's why you need to spend as much time as necessary in this first chapter to get your track laid for that masterpiece that is crying out to be written. Before you ever get to the opening sentence of that masterpiece you first have to write the most important sentence of all—the sentence that summarizes your manuscript and will serve to keep it on track throughout your entire journey of writing the piece. That way, if you lose focus while writing the manuscript, you'll realize it when the ride begins to get bumpy and you look up to find that you're in danger of going nowhere because you're no longer on track. At that point you stop what you're writing, turn around, and get back to going in the right direction once again.

Here are some tips to get you started in laying your track. Ask yourself these questions, and then write your answers in the spaces given. (If working in a group, pair off and discuss your answers.)

- What first gave me the idea to write this piece?

_____

_____

_____

_____

- Why is it important to me to write it?

  _____

  _____

  _____

  _____

- What do I want others to "take away" after reading it?

  _____

  _____

  _____

  _____

Your answers to these questions will be crucial in laying your track through the writing of your one-sentence statement. Once you've considered these questions and answers, go ahead and start formulating your statement on the lines below. You will probably want to experiment with several one-sentence statements before you decide on the one that's just right. (If working in a group, get back with the partner you've been working with so far and bounce ideas off each other before writing them down.)

  _____

  _____

  _____

  _____

  _____

  _____

When you've come up with what you consider to be the final draft of your one-sentence statement, the next step—assuming you're serious about actually writing this masterpiece that's in your heart—is to type or write that statement in very large, bold letters on a piece of paper and then post it where you can see it every time you work on your manuscript. Again, I call this "laying the track" because as you work on constructing your word train you will have the statement right in front of you to remind you of the theme of your piece and to keep you from getting off-track. Once your track is successfully laid—written down and prominently displayed where you can easily see it each time you start writing—then you will be ready to move on to chapter two, where we will talk about "cow catchers" and "snowplows" and "grabbers," as we begin work on constructing the train itself.

Chapter Two

"The Cow Catcher"

"They threw me off the hay truck about noon."

That is the opening line of James M. Cain's *The Postman Always Rings Twice*. Did it get your attention? Did it grab you, intrigue you, suck you immediately into the story and make you want to read on? If so, then you've just been snagged by a cow catcher.

Now don't get me wrong. I'm not inferring that you're some sort of bovine creature. What I am saying is that you've just been hooked by a first-class writer who knows how to start a book. Let's look at some other famous—and some not so famous, but all intriguing—opening lines.

- On February 8, 1956, in a little chapel in Loretto, Pennsylvania, I was ambushed by Jesus of Nazareth. —*Abba's Child* by Brennan Manning

- There once was a boy by the name of Eustace Clarence Scrubb, and he almost deserved it. —*The Voyage of the Dawn Treader* by C. S. Lewis

- It was the best of times, it was the worst of times. —*A Tale of Two Cities* by Charles Dickens

- Elmer Gantry was drunk. —*Elmer Gantry* by Sinclair Lewis

- I had this story from one who had no business to tell it to me, or to any other…. —*Tarzan of the Apes* by Edgar Rice Burroughs

- "Tom!" —*Adventures of Tom Sawyer* by Mark Twain

- The cracking sound of gunfire exploded behind them, continuing for several seconds before Melissa and Carrie, en route to the auditorium with dozens of other students, realized there was a problem. —*The Price* by Kathi Mills-Macias

These captivating openers, or "cow catchers," are designed to hook readers and get them into the story that follows. And though that has always been a crucial component of good writing, it is even more important today when we find ourselves living in a culture of "sound bites," populated by scores of people with short attention spans who require sensational visuals to attract and maintain their interest.

Let's face it. We now live, for the most part, in a high tech world where movies, television, and video games are quickly replacing reading as a favorite pastime. In fact, I remember hearing not long ago that the average American reads at a sixth grade level, and fewer and fewer people are reading at all, except for required business or related studies. And though I personally find that very sad, I can't change it. All I can do is work that much harder at fine-tuning and honing my own writing in an attempt to attract and hold as many readers as possible, knowing that I'm competing for their valuable time with star-studded, action-packed, multi-million dollar visuals and bleeping, flashing, virtual-reality cyber games.

And so we come back to the cow catcher, a term that is so outdated in today's culture that there are few people left who have even the remotest idea of what I'm talking about. So for those of you who, unlike me, aren't yet quite as old as dirt, let me explain.

Years ago, long before trains were streamlined, the old steam engines were built with a sort of metal grating in front, down near the tracks, in order to "scoop up" a cow—or any other unwelcome varmint, for that matter—that might be loitering on the track, and then carry it along until the train was able to come safely to a stop. The cow might or might not survive the scooping, but it certainly had a better chance than if the train had just plowed right into it—not to mention the damage the cow could do to the train itself, including any passengers who might be on board. Cow catchers were also known as snowplows because the metal device could be used in a similar way to scoop up large piles or drifts of snow from the track so the train's progress wouldn't be impeded. But for our purposes, we're just going to stick with calling these necessary and highly functional front-of-the-engine devices cow catchers.

Now to be fair, I will admit there are times that you simply need more than one sentence to build an effective cow catcher for your train—two or three, possibly, maybe even four, but certainly no more than a very brief paragraph. Let's look at a couple more cow catchers, this time requiring more than one sentence to get the train moving.

***

You know how it is there early in the morning in Havana with the bums still asleep against the walls of the buildings; before even the ice wagons come by with ice for the bars? Well, we came across the square from the dock to the Pearl of San Francisco Café to get coffee and there was only one beggar awake in the square and he was getting a drink out of the fountain. But when we got inside the café and sat down, there were the three of them waiting for us. —*To Have and Have Not* by Ernest Hemingway

***

Do you see how Hemingway not only gave us the geographical setting for the story (Havana) and the time of day (early morning), but he also painted a vivid image of the street scene itself, replete with colorful characters (the bums asleep against the walls of the buildings and the beggar getting a drink from the fountain) and a feeling of anticipation that something important is about to happen (three of "them" were waiting for the main characters to come into the café). The setting raises all sorts of questions, all of which beg to be answered: What is about to happen? Something good? Something bad? Who are "them" and who are "us"? In one paragraph we know the where and when of the opening scene, and we care about the characters and what is going to happen to them. That is brilliant writing, as is the following.

***

She gave a startled cry. "What's the matter?" he asked. Notwithstanding the darkness of the shuttered room he saw her face on a sudden distraught with terror. "Someone just tried the door." —*Painted Veil* by Somerset Maugham

***

Here we have an extremely short paragraph, consisting of three brief sentences and one slightly longer. Yet within these four sentences we are immediately drawn into a shuttered room with just enough light for the man in the story to see the woman's face. We know the woman is scared because she gives a startled cry and the man understands from her expression that she is terrified. We also get the feeling that, whatever the relationship between the two in the room—husband and wife, lovers, friends, relatives, or even something less—the man, to one degree or another, cares for the woman. Finally, we are left with a feeling of dread and imminent danger because someone is trying to break in, though we may wonder why the woman noticed it and the man did not. Let's try another one.

***

As the tune played inside my head, gunfire exploded in the cramped underground space around me. My eyes flew up as muscle, bone, and guts splattered against rock just three feet from me. The mangled body seemed glued for a moment, then slid downward, leaving a smear of blood and hair. — *Monday Mourning* by Kathy Reichs

***

Here we have a rather gruesome but clearly descriptive opening to a murder mystery, though the next paragraph goes on to explain that the bloody massacre witnessed by the character in the opening scene is actually that of another character killing a very large rat. However, limiting ourselves to the opening paragraph, we don't know that. What we do know is that the character introduced in this opening paragraph had a song going through his/her head, though we don't know if that character is male or female, old or young, good or evil, handsome or homely, fat or thin, or what in the world he/she is doing in such an awful predicament. Those details are simply not important in grabbing the reader's immediate attention. The graphic description of what was going on around the character is the key. We can almost hear the exploding gunfire as it drowns out the tune in the character's mind, and we are nearly claustrophobic as we imagine the confined underground space. Yet we know it wasn't totally dark in that space because the character clearly describes the carnage that takes place a mere three feet in front of him/her. It would be a rare reader who would put down the book after reading such a powerful cow catcher. Okay, here's one more.

***

It was a rare golden autumn day in the Pacific Northwest that my then two-year-old son, Chris, taught me the meaning of faith. I had taken him to the park for a picnic, and as I unloaded the car, he ran on ahead, looking for the playground. Suddenly I sensed that something was very wrong. — "Ask and Receive" by Kathi (Mills) Macias

***

This story opens with an idyllic setting—a mother and her toddler, in the normally rainy Pacific Northwest, taking advantage of a rare sunny autumn day to go to the park for a picnic. All seems peaceful as the mother unloads the car and prepares to follow her child, who has run on ahead to the playground. Then, into that pristine picture comes a hint of danger as a mother's instincts kick in. Because the first sentences establish the main characters as a loving mother and her innocent two-year-old, the readers immediately care about them and don't want anything bad to happen, though it seems likely that some sort of tragedy is about to strike. Once again, the readers are driven to read on to be sure all turns out well for the little family.

All of these cow catchers consisted of more than one sentence, yet they were still brief and definitely attention-getters. Holding that thought, I want you now to consider your own masterpiece for a moment. Assuming that you've already laid your track in the previous chapter, it's time to prepare your cow catcher.

First, look again at your track, that one-sentence statement that catches the heart or takeaway of your piece. Read it—and then read it again, several times. Now close your eyes and see if you can transfer that statement to a visual in your mind. Think Technicolor here, no black and whites. Let your visual come to life, let it breathe, let it begin to speak to you until you catch at least one phrase (more, if possible) that seems appropriate as a cow catcher. Then jot it/them down on the lines below. Remember, we're just looking for key phrases, not the finalized cow catcher.

_____

_____

_____

_____

_____

_____

Now I want you to read that phrase out loud, as many times as necessary—and *listen* to your words. If you're working in a group, get together with your partner—if possible, the same one you've been working with all along—and read the phrase(s) out loud several times to each other, then discuss the following questions:

- What is there about the phrase(s) that excites/motivates you?

- How can you build on that point to construct the powerful grabber you need to open your piece and catch your readers' attention?

Look with me for a moment at the opening sentence in my book *The Price*, which I quoted earlier in this chapter. I'll repeat it here to refresh your memory: "The cracking sound of gunfire exploded behind them, continuing for several seconds before Melissa and Carrie, en route to the auditorium with dozens of other students, realized there was a problem."

This entire novel revolves around a school shooting and its aftermath, with two of the primary characters being a couple of teenaged girls named Melissa and Carrie, who just happen to be lifelong best friends. My goal as I opened the story was to grab the readers' attention with a dramatic statement that would not only set the scene for the book but would also cause the readers to care about and identify with these two teenagers. In one sentence I have established the setting as a school, and have named only Melissa and Carrie out of all the students heading for the auditorium, therefore implying the two girls' importance in the book. In addition, the use of such colorful and descriptive words as "cracking" and "exploded" helps to paint a sharp picture that the readers can easily transfer from the words on the page to a visual in their minds. The readers also get the impression in that one opening sentence that, even as Melissa and Carrie become aware of what is going on around them, the shooting is continuing, so the two girls, as well as all the other students, are still in grave danger. The personal introduction of these two young girls, who seem to be key players in the unfolding drama, combined with the implication that they are in imminent danger, is a sure hook to reel the readers into the story.

All right, are you ready to try a couple of trial runs before tackling your own masterpiece? If so, I'm going to give you some examples of factual yet drab, lifeless openings, and then you see if you can turn them into some real grabbers by rewriting them in the spaces provided. Remember, there are no right and wrong answers here, as each of you will write these in your own words and from your own perspective, but I will give you my own version of the rewritten opening after you've had a chance to write yours. (For those of you working in a group, time to get together with your partners again.)

***

My name is Mary, and I have a grown son named John. John has always seemed a bit different from the other kids, but I got very upset with our youth pastor a few years ago when he took it upon himself to point out that fact to me. I really didn't think it was any of his business. Deep down, however, I sensed that he was right.

***

_____

_____

_____

_____

_____

_____

How did you do? Just for comparison, here is my version (which, by the way, is the version that was printed when this particular article appeared in *Home Life* magazine in 1991).

***

"Mary, have you ever realized that John is different from other kids?" When the youth pastor at our church asked me that question many years ago, I was insulted. How dare he imply there was something wrong with my son! But even then I believe I knew what he was hinting at—I just couldn't bring myself to admit it. — "Welcome Home, John" by Mary Read as told to Kathi (Mills) Macias

***

Can you see the difference? Can you feel it? The first example gave the facts, but left out the feeling, violating one of the most important guidelines of good writing: Show, don't tell. Anyone can relay facts, but it takes a seasoned writer to show those facts by painting a word picture.

Okay, let's try another one.

***

When I was young I used to think I wanted to have lots of children when I grew up. Each time I told my mother about it, she always told me I wasn't being very realistic.

***

_____

_____

_____

_____

_____

_____

And now here is my rewrite. This one is the opening to a story called "Parenting: The Guilt that Keeps on Growing," taken from my book *Confessions from the Far Side of Thirty*.

***

As a little girl, I used to make inane comments like, "When I grow up I'm going to have nine kids!" My mother would just look at me, horrified, and say things like, "Well, if you do, it'll serve you right."

***

Are you getting the picture? Good, because now it's your turn to paint a picture. This time you're going to construct the cow catcher for your own masterpiece. Focus on the fact that you are going to do the exact opposite of what you want your readers to do, which is to transfer the words on the page to a visual in their mind. Your job, as you do this final exercise in this chapter, is to transfer the visual in your mind to words on the page—sharp, clear, colorful, powerful words that will grab and entice your readers. Think of it as a sort of visual exchange, from your mind to the readers', with your words being the medium of exchange. In essence, through the constructing of your cow catcher you are inviting the readers to join you on a word journey that, as they read, will become their journey as well as yours. Your invitation must therefore be compelling—an offer that's just too good to refuse.

Are you ready? Okay, give it a try. And remember, just as it was with laying your track in the previous chapter, you will probably need to construct several cow catchers and make lots of revisions before you come up with the perfect opening for your masterpiece. (If working in a group, get back with your partner once again and work through the construction of your cow catchers together, comparing notes back and forth as you brainstorm and write.)

_____

_____

_____

_____

_____

_____

There it is—the opening sentence, or sentences, of your manuscript. Can you see how the masterpiece that has been burning inside you for so long is finally beginning to come to life? The track is laid and the opening grabber is on paper. Now it's time to move on to the next big step—building on the cow catcher to construct the locomotive so we can finally get this train moving in the right direction.

Chapter Three

"The Locomotive"

Ever since I was a child the call of a locomotive wailing in the distance as it headed for parts unknown has tugged at the strings of my heart—and I imagine I'm not the only one who has had that experience. There's just something about that plaintive cry that woos us to drop what we're doing, run as fast as we can, and hop aboard for a serendipitous ride. And, of course, that's exactly what we want our locomotive to do for our readers as we invite them along on our journey of words.

The difference, however, is that we've already wooed our potential readers with a cow catcher. We've "snatched" them up, if you will, and now it's our responsibility to give them a fairly clear idea of where we're taking them. What can they expect to experience on this trip? Will it be a romantic ride through pleasant scenery, a frightening one through dark and unknown territory, a humorous journey with colorful fellow passengers, or maybe all of the above? Will it be a learning experience, or simply an entertaining diversion? Will it challenge their intellect, their values, or maybe even their sense of safety and security? Is it a journey they will want to take alone, or should they consider sharing it with a companion? All of these are valid questions, and we need to give our readers enough answers early on so they can make a decision as to whether or not they want to continue on the trip. And that, of course, is why we must make our locomotive as appealing as possible.

Now this doesn't mean that before we've even pulled out of the station we have to reveal all that will take place during the entire journey; there's always room for surprises and even an occasional detour (so long as it is relevant to the story and doesn't get us off track) as the trip progresses. But it is essential that our readers get a clear sense of what they've signed up for before we attempt to take them any farther.

With that in mind, let's start constructing our locomotive by expanding on some of our cow catchers from the previous chapter. The first one is from the as-told-to article I wrote and published in *Home Life* in January 1991. The title is "Welcome Home, John," and you'll recognize the two opening paragraphs from one of the exercises you worked on before writing your own cow catcher.

***

"Mary, have you ever realized that John is different from other kids?"

When the youth pastor at our church asked me that question many years ago, I was insulted. How dare he imply there was something wrong with my son! But even then I believe I knew what he was hinting at—I just couldn't bring myself to admit it.

As the years passed, however, my husband, Bob, and I had to deal with the revelation that our oldest child, John, was a practicing homosexual. As conservative, evangelical Christians who knew and believed what the Bible said on the subject of homosexuality, this was an agonizing realization.

Besides being homosexual John was heavily involved in drugs and alcohol. He moved in and out of our home countless times throughout the years, never really feeling he "belonged" anywhere.

Then just when we thought we, as a family, had begun to deal with John's homosexuality, he got sick. He woke up at night drenched with sweat. He was back and forth to doctors with an assortment of vague ailments, none seemingly connected. Then I came across an article in *Newsweek* about a relatively new and deadly disease—AIDS.

***

All right, you've read the locomotive for "Welcome Home, John." What did you learn from it? Did you get a relatively good feel for where the article is going? Who are the main characters in the article? What is happening in their lives? What is the impending point of conflict or tragedy that will need to be addressed and/or resolved before the journey's end? Readers can easily conclude from these five paragraphs that the locomotive is taking them on a ride that will involve a young man who was raised in a conservative Christian home, yet is living a lifestyle at odds with his parents' values and has more than likely contracted what was, at that time, an almost unheard of yet deadly disease. The readers, of course, don't yet know how the story will play out—whether John and his parents will come to an understanding and resolution of their differences; whether the story will carry through all the way to John's death; whether John will finally find a place he belongs, and if so where that might be—but they know those are the issues that will more than likely be addressed, to one extent or another. In short, the readers know enough to decide whether or not they want to stay on the train for the entire ride or jump off at the next stop.

Before we attempt to expand on your own cow catcher and construct the locomotive for your train, let's build on another cow catcher from the previous chapter, this time from my suspense novel *The Price*. If you remember this was a one-sentence cow catcher, and now we will look at the rest of the opening section of the book, the part that comprises the locomotive.

***

The cracking sound of gunfire exploded behind them, continuing for several seconds before Melissa and Carrie, en route to the auditorium with dozens of other students, realized there was a problem. As scattered screams joined the staccato barrage, Melissa stopped in her tracks and turned back toward the sound. Her wide green eyes took in the surrealistic scene even as its reality began to register in her brain. Teenagers—some of them her friends, others known only by sight—stood, for the most part frozen in fear and disbelief, while a few others bolted for the nearest exits. Then she saw him—the vaguely familiar face, terrifying in its calm resolve, the gloved hands holding the assault rifle in front of him as he fired into the crowd.

Suddenly, amid the escalating screams and gunfire, Melissa heard a moan. Willing herself to turn away from the horrifying drama unfolding in front of her, she looked down. There, lying at her feet, was Carrie, her skin so white it seemed grayish-green against the crimson pool spreading from beneath her twisted young body. It was then that Melissa's screams escaped from somewhere deep within as she fell to the floor beside the seemingly lifeless girl who had been her closest friend for as long as she could remember.

***

Our example of a locomotive here is a bit longer than the previous example, but there's a very good reason for that. The first example was taken from a magazine article, while this one was used as the opening for a novel. We have a lot more room to develop our locomotive for a book than we do for an article or short story; in fact, the example from *The Price* is actually quite short for a book-length locomotive. Some books may require several pages to effectively construct the locomotive that will accurately portray to the readers where this particular word journey will take them. In *The Price*, however, I felt that brevity and jolting clarity were essential to set the tone and pace of the story.

And just what is that tone and pace? What did you sense as you read those opening paragraphs? We saw in the previous chapter, as we examined the first sentence, that the story was about two teenaged girls who were caught in the middle of a high school shooting. Now, of course, we know a bit more, and we have a stronger sense of where the story is going.

First, we see the scene unfolding through the eyes of Melissa, who has turned back to see what was happening. We sense her horrified yet detached assessment of the situation, as she catches sight of other students around her—some, like her, too shocked to move, while others attempt to flee the slaughter. We also discover that the gloved shooter is calmly firing an assault rifle into the crowd, and that he appears vaguely familiar to Melissa, presenting the possibility that he may be someone she knows, or at least has met, possibly even another student.

Next we see Melissa's attention torn from the shooter to her companion, Carrie, who has apparently been hit by one or more stray bullets and is now lying at Melissa's feet. Her condition appears grave, possibly even fatal. It is the sight of her friend that causes Melissa to make the transition from her detached state to her first display of grief, as she realizes that she may have lost her lifelong best friend.

Finally, we recognize that some very serious questions are going to have to be addressed in the book: Will Carrie live or die? If she lives, what will be her condition and how will she deal with it? How will Carrie's fate affect Melissa? Who was the shooter, and what drove him to commit such a violent crime? Will he be captured, tried, convicted? Did he operate alone, or did he have one or more accomplices? How will his fate affect the other students, particularly Melissa? And, of course, regardless of what happens to anyone else in the book, it is at least implied that Melissa will more than likely continue to be one of the main characters on this journey.

Having learned that much and having been confronted by many questions from the opening paragraphs of the book, the readers now know enough to decide whether or not they want to stay onboard for the remainder of the ride. Assuming it is the type of story they enjoy and that I, as the author, have properly constructed my locomotive, they very well may choose to do so.

To illustrate how versatile this train-of-thought writing method can be, let's apply it to a children's story called "Taking a Chance" from the book *Life Can Be Tough*, one of my two children's anthologies. As you read through these opening paragraphs, note that the first paragraph is actually the cow catcher, but it flows right into the next six paragraphs, which together make up the locomotive.

***

When Annie Browning's third grade teacher, Mrs. Jackson, decided it was time to move the desks around, Annie found herself sitting right next to Elizabeth. Annie wasn't very happy about that. Everybody knew Elizabeth was stuck-up. Besides, Elizabeth was different from everyone else in the classroom. Her skin was dark, and all the kids said it was because Elizabeth was from another country.

Annie was glad she wasn't from another country. She hoped Mrs. Jackson would move the desks again real soon.

What happened instead was that Mrs. Jackson gave the class an assignment to do in pairs, and Annie was paired with Elizabeth. Annie didn't like that at all. She didn't think Elizabeth liked it either because she hardly talked to her while they worked. But Annie had to admit that Elizabeth did a pretty good job. And when Mrs. Jackson gave them an A on the assignment, Elizabeth smiled a big smile at Annie. Annie was really surprised about that.

The next morning Elizabeth smiled at Annie again as they walked into the classroom. This time Annie smiled back. *Maybe Elizabeth's not so stuck-up after all*, she thought.

When the bell rang to go to lunch Annie hurried to get a good seat next to her friends in the cafeteria. They were all laughing and having a good time when Annie looked up and saw Elizabeth walking toward them, carrying her lunch tray.

Annie started to smile at Elizabeth, but then Heather, who was sitting next to Annie, saw Elizabeth, too. "Oh, no," Heather said in a loud voice, "here comes that stuck-up Elizabeth. I sure hope she doesn't think she's going to sit with us."

Everyone laughed. Annie tried to laugh too, but she couldn't. She just looked down at her plate. When she looked up again, she saw that Elizabeth had stuck her nose up in the air and walked right past their table. Annie decided her friends were right about Elizabeth—she really was stuck-up!

***

Adults reading these opening paragraphs could easily surmise that the story is going to be about Annie's coming to a place of realizing that Elizabeth really isn't stuck-up at all, but rather is trying to protect herself from being hurt by the unkind remarks of her classmates. Annie will also realize that Elizabeth's skin coloring and nationality do not mean that she's different inside from other children. Having come to those realizations Annie will then have to choose whether or not to stand up to her friends, risking their rejection and disapproval in order to defend Elizabeth. However, keeping in mind that this story was written for children aged six to ten, it is safe to assume that they may not realize all that from these few paragraphs. Yet, if the facts have been presented in a setting to which young readers can relate, they will want to stay onboard to see what happens to Annie and Elizabeth as their journey continues.

For our final example let's look at one of my nonfiction books, *Mommy, Where Are You?* Again, the opening paragraph is the cow catcher; the following nine paragraphs complete the locomotive.

***

Mother's Day, 1954. I had just turned six. My palms were sweaty, my bony knees were knocking, and my heart was pounding in my ears, as I awaited my turn to stand up and announce to the entire kindergarten class, along with a sizable group of very proud mothers, why I loved my mom.

"I love my mom because she's soft when I sit on her lap," one little girl whispered shyly, as embarrassed giggles engulfed the other children.

"I love my mom because she bakes me cookies," declared the freckle-faced boy across the aisle.

"I love my mom because she doesn't make me take naps anymore," added the curly-haired girl in front of me.

And then it was my turn.

"I...I love my mom because..." I stopped, horrified. I knew I loved my mom, and I knew there were a hundred reasons why I did, but for the life of me I couldn't think of any one of them.

I turned and looked at the group of mothers seated in the back of the classroom. They were all smiling at me encouragingly, but my mom's smile was the biggest of the bunch. And definitely the most beautiful. That's when I remembered.

"I love my mom because she takes care of me when I'm sick," I said, then added, "and that's a lot!"

As I sat back down, I didn't even mind the giggles sweeping across the room because I knew I had thought of just the right reason why I loved my mom. A frail, asthmatic child, I had already logged more sick time in my six short years than most people do in a lifetime. But no matter how sick I was or how long I had to stay in bed, I could always count on one thing: Mom would be right there by my side.

That was 1954. It was a lot more common—and a lot easier—for moms to be at their children's side then than it is today. Kids growing up in that era were part of the "Donna Reed/Ozzie and Harriet/Father Knows Best" generation. We didn't have to watch "Happy Days" on TV because we were living them. (Besides, we got only one channel on our black-and-white TV, and the most exciting thing that was ever on was wrestling or the test pattern.) When we called out, "Mommy, where are you?" we would hear her answer, "I'm in the kitchen, honey, making your lunch." But when our children or our children's children call out, "Mommy, where are you?" they are likely to hear a daycare worker inform them, "Mommy's at work. She'll pick you up at 5:30, just like she always does. Now go play with the other children."

***

Speaking in the first person, I used my own experience as a nervous six-year-old to draw in the readers and to map out their planned trip. Without too much guesswork readers can now assume that this book is probably directed to mothers of young children, most of whom are valiantly struggling to juggle their many and various responsibilities, including home, family, and career. Though readers may not yet know where I, as the author, stand on the subject or what my advice or counsel will be, they at least know enough to decide whether or not the subject is of sufficient interest to them to read on.

Using what you've gleaned from these four examples of locomotives, it's time to begin constructing your own locomotive. First, revisit your track, the sentence that is the foundation for your entire piece. Then reread your cow catcher, keeping in mind that your locomotive will flow from the cow catcher, as you saw in the previous four examples in this chapter. Then, in the blank spaces provided below, jot down the thoughts that you feel are vital to the construction of your locomotive, those elements that will enable your readers to get a good idea of where their journey is going to take them. Don't worry about trying to get these thoughts in perfect writing order; just get them down, and then you can reorganize and rewrite them in the next step. (This is the time to get with your partner, if you've been working with one, and brainstorm together as you complete this exercise.)

_____

_____

_____

_____

_____

_____

All right, now that you're clear on the points you want to include in your locomotive it's time to start the actual writing. Rather than include the blank spaces here in the book, since you probably will need a lot of space for rewrites before you accomplish your task, I would suggest you begin this major part of your writing on a computer, word processor, or typewriter. Though some of you may want to continue to work in pairs on this exercise, most writers find they work best in solitude. You can always get together with your partner after you're done and compare notes then, at which point you may find that you'll want to do another revision or two.

Once you feel satisfied with your locomotive, it will be time to move on to the next part of the train—the boxcars. This will entail the bulk of your work, as it constitutes the body of your writing. It will be the most challenging and time-consuming part of your project, but the most exciting and rewarding as well, as you see your masterpiece finally becoming a reality. Therefore it's important to spend as much time as necessary in this chapter before moving on to the next.

Chapter Four

"The Boxcars"

Though it is quickly becoming a lost art (and I use the term *very* loosely), do you remember sitting in the family automobile at a railroad crossing and counting the boxcars as they rolled by? I certainly do. My brothers and I would drive our parents crazy as we counted aloud from the backseat, beginning with the car immediately following the locomotive and continuing all the way to the final car just before the caboose: "One…two…three…" It wasn't unusual to reach 100 cars and still be counting, though I don't doubt that my parents prayed fervently for shorter trains.

And that is an extremely important point to keep in mind as we begin to construct the main body of our train: no unnecessary boxcars! Though we don't want to make our train too short and leave out something important, neither do we want to commit the unpardonable sin of boring our readers with *too much information*. My goal is to have my readers come away from my books saying, "I hated for that story to come to an end. I can't wait to read the next one." The last thing I want one of my readers to say is, "I tried to get through it but it just kept dragging on…."

Proper construction and organization of boxcars is crucial to the efficiency and power of your train. Here are the instructions I give to the students in my classroom when we get to the boxcar section of my course on train-of-thought writing: Take a pen and as many blank pieces of paper as necessary, then find a comfortable place to sit where you have room to spread out in all directions. (Most opt for the floor, but I'll leave that up to you.) Then begin to think through your manuscript from start to finish. What is the first logical point you want to make following your locomotive? If you're writing the life story of Albert Einstein and have given an inviting overview of it in your cow catcher/ locomotive section, you may want your first point after that to be a brief history of his birth and family background. This would then be your first boxcar. The second point may take your readers into his early years and the first signs of his unusual intelligence, while the third could cover his emergence as a genius while his peers struggled through plane geometry and elementary physics, etc. (I have chosen a simple example to explain this part of the process; most manuscripts won't follow such an obvious progression, but this should help you get started with the logical progression of your own masterpiece.)

As you identify these progressive points you need to give each point a title and write it on a separate piece of paper, keeping in mind that each piece of paper represents a boxcar. Underneath that title you will need to come up with a one-sentence summary of that point, as well as some sub-points to reinforce your main point. For instance, using the simplistic example in the previous paragraph, if your first point following the locomotive that will carry the readers through Einstein's life story is his birth, you might temporarily (for your own use) title that boxcar "Einstein's Birth and Family Background." Underneath that title you could write a simple explanation of the point, such as "the story of his birth family and the day he joined them." You could then list some sub-points to include in that boxcar, such as "how his parents met"; "financial situation of family"; "how his birth immediately affected his family," etc.

In a short story or a book of fiction, assuming you are clear on your overall plot or storyline, you may have a relatively simple time figuring out the most logical and effective order of your manuscript, whereas in a nonfiction article or book you may know only that you want to cover certain points pertaining to your chosen topic but not be particularly clear on the best order for those points. That's where the separate pieces of paper, or boxcars, come in handy, and why you need room to spread them out. Once you have identified and written down your points on these separate pieces of paper you can begin to spread your boxcars out around you in what seems to be the most logical order. If you've been collaborating with another writer on this project, you will find that a pair of objective eyes can often spot an obvious omission that you, as a sole author, might be too close to see. Together you can attempt to track the smooth and logical progression of your manuscript from boxcar to boxcar, checking for omissions as well as possible changes of order. (I have seen students attempt this process and end up with their sheets of paper in a completely different order than what they had originally envisioned.)

Before you get started on your own boxcars, let's look at a couple of brief examples from my own writing. The first is a short chapter from my nonfiction humor book, *Confessions from the Far Side of Thirty*. The chapter's title is "Excuse Me, Ma'am." (The paragraphs are numbered for convenience.)

***

1"Paper or plastic, ma'am? Ma'am? Excuse me, ma'am?"

2Do you know what a shock it is the first time you realize that the bag boy (or is that bag person? I'm almost sure it's not bag lady) at the grocery store is addressing you as "ma'am"? I mean, it doesn't seem that long ago when my mother was teaching me to respect my elders—and now I am one!

3It's a strange feeling, isn't it? True, the term "ma'am" is meant to convey respect, but it's hard to keep that in mind when hearing it makes you feel as old as Methuselah.

4But I have a theory. It isn't that I'm as old as the people I used to refer to as "ma'am" and "sir"; it's that people are now being born at a much younger age.

5Think about it. When was the last time you checked out the age of a fireman or a policeman or an ambulance driver? Surely they don't allow them to participate in these professions before the age of fourteen, and yet none of the ones I've seen lately looked old enough to shave.

₆I used to laugh at my elderly neighbor's story of "that young whippersnapper of a policeman, still wet behind the ears," who had pulled her over for driving too slowly.

₇"Why, I told him I didn't need any advice from him," she explained. "After all, I was driving before he was born."

₈He must have been impressed with her logic because he let her go with only a warning—which she ignored completely.

₉But now I'm beginning to think maybe she was right. I mean, they're graduating those guys from the police academy younger and younger all the time. (I wonder if that's why some of them ride bikes instead of driving cars—they're simply not old enough to get a driver's license.)

₁₀The worst thing, however, is when you go to the doctor and he looks like he just blew in from an after-school sock hop. (Okay, so I'm exaggerating. But braces on a surgeon do not inspire confidence, believe me. And when he has to call his mother before he can schedule an operation, I'm outta there!)

₁₁Let's face it. We baby boomers are middle-aged people living in a youth-oriented world. And if we're not careful we'll get sucked right into their mindset. If we do that, we'll waste the best years of our lives reminiscing about the "good old days."

₁₂Be truthful. What was so good about being young? Would you really want to be a teenager again? (I'd rather eat cat food.) Besides, it only takes about ten years to get used to how old you are, so be patient.

₁₃Personally I'm inclined to agree with the English poet Robert Browning, who penned these famous lines:

Grow old along with me! The best is yet to be

The last of life, for which the first was made;

Our times are in His hand.

14With that in mind, it doesn't hurt so much to be called "ma'am." In fact, I think I kind of like it!

***

All right, by now you've had enough experience with cow catchers and locomotives to identify those train sections in the three opening paragraphs. We know from those paragraphs that this is a piece about my struggles with making the transition from youth to middle-age (and beyond). Paragraph four, however, introduces the first boxcar in the manuscript: my "theory" that people are now being born at a younger age. The next six paragraphs are actually a part of that same boxcar of thought, expanding and reinforcing my theory through the use of four examples (the sub-points I mentioned earlier):

- Emergency workers look younger
- Elderly neighbor's experience with a policeman
- Policemen on bicycles
- Doctors wearing braces

The next boxcar begins at paragraph eleven, where I move from my ludicrous theory that people are being born at an earlier age to the simple fact that we are living in a youth-oriented culture. This, of course, is news to no one, but it is a reminder to those who relate to my struggles with aging that our struggles are not unfounded or unreasonable. However, I then challenge the readers with the thought that getting old really isn't such a bad thing after all. And that's the focus of the second boxcar, which extends through paragraph thirteen, including these sub-points:

- Don't waste today reminiscing about the "good old days"
- Being young isn't all it's cracked up to be
- The last of our days can be the best

Finally, the piece wraps up with a positive statement in paragraph fourteen (our caboose, which we will discuss in the final chapter).

Obviously this is a relatively short train, with only two boxcars, but then it's a relatively short piece of writing. The construction and purpose of the train, however, is simple to observe. Those two lone boxcars serve to carry the readers smoothly from the locomotive, which states my struggles with aging (negative), to the resolution of the problem, found in the caboose, which declares my peace with and acceptance of the aging process (positive).

Let's look at one more example. This is an article called "The Reluctant Reunion," written and published decades ago when my writing career was just taking off—dragging me reluctantly into the speaking aspect of that career.

***

1"You want me to do *what*?" I gasped, clutching the receiver tightly as a wave of nausea swept over me.

2A familiar panic gripped my throat as he repeated his invitation. "It's just that I've been following your writing career lately, and I wondered if you would come and speak to my students. It would be a great encouragement to them."

3I closed my eyes and breathed a desperate prayer. Although I had been pleasantly surprised when I picked up the phone to hear the voice of Bob Ferris, my former high school English and creative writing teacher, I had no idea that he was about to ask me to speak to a group of students.

4I swallowed hard. "When do you want me to come?"

5"How about next Thursday morning—about nine-thirty?"

6My mind was reeling. "Next Thursday? That soon?"

7"Yes, if you can. You see, our annual writing contest is coming up next month. I thought, since you did so well in it years ago, you might be a real inspiration to the kids."

8He seemed to know all the right things to say. As I groped frantically for a legitimate excuse, I realized I couldn't possibly say no.

9"Sure," I answered meekly. "I'd be glad to."

10It was one of the biggest lies I'd ever told.

11I spent the entire next week trying to find a way out of my commitment, but to no avail. To make matters worse, everyone I mentioned it to immediately congratulated me on the wonderful opportunity and told me how exciting it would be to return to my former high school as a successful writer. "It'll be just like a reunion," they offered. "And everybody loves reunions!"

12*Not everyone*, I thought. *Especially when they involve public speaking....*

13The day arrived all too quickly. I drove up to the high school and sat in my car, trying to convince myself to get out. When I could put it off no longer, I stepped out of the car and walked on shaky legs across the familiar campus.

14My mouth was dry and there was a faint buzzing in my ears as I opened the door to the classroom. Mr. Ferris grinned and gave me a bear hug as I walked in. But as I looked at the students, with their bizarre clothes and hairdos, I knew I'd made a big mistake. Their expressions seemed hostile—at best, passive and disinterested.

15Wishing I could turn and run back to my car, I instead forced myself to walk to the front of the room. Somehow I made it through my brief presentation without fainting. When I asked if there were any questions, the only sound I could hear was my own heart, pounding in my ears. Clasping my sweaty hands together to keep them from shaking, I smiled woodenly for what seemed an eternity. Finally, my face hot with embarrassment, I mumbled a weak "thanks" and hurried to the back of the room, where I sank down into an empty chair.

16Suddenly I realized someone was speaking to me. I turned to see a slightly overweight boy with a severe case of acne, sitting in a desk in the next row and staring at me shyly as he asked a question.

17I could have kissed him! Instead I repeated his question to the rest of the class, then proceeded to answer it as accurately as I could. I had no sooner finished than someone else called out a question—and then another and another. With each question I answered, my confidence grew.

18Before long one girl asked if I would be willing to look at her work. Soon I was thrilled by the number of students wanting to talk with me. They quietly lined up and waited, clutching their manuscripts, eager to show me what they had written. As I read I realized they were showing me more than just their writing—they were allowing me to catch a glimpse of their hopes, dreams, disappointments, and pain. And I felt as though I had read those papers somewhere before—in fact, that I had lived them.

19When I looked up into their anxious faces, nervously awaiting my response to their work, I no longer saw the strange clothes, the weird hairdos, and the overdone makeup. I saw myself, so many years earlier, striving, failing, searching, growing.

20*Growing.* I smiled to myself. *Still growing....*

21I left the classroom with several addresses and phone numbers of students who had asked me to keep in touch. As I walked back down the corridors, there was a bounce in my step, and I realized that what had started out as a rather reluctant reunion had actually blossomed into a triumphant one.

***

Again, the cow catcher and locomotive are obvious in this article. The first paragraph, the cow catcher, expresses my frantic reaction to what I'd just heard. The next two paragraphs complete the locomotive, clarifying the invitation I'd received and expanding on my reaction to it. The readers now have a good sense of where this journey will take them.

The first boxcar begins in paragraph four and carries through to paragraph twelve. In these paragraphs the readers move past my initial emotional reaction and begin to see my actual response, which is a reluctant acceptance of the invitation and a week's agonizing over my need to carry through on it. The sub-points in this boxcar are:

- Date and time of engagement
- Verbal acceptance of invitation
- Agonizing over decision and dreading carrying it out

Boxcar number two runs from paragraphs thirteen through fifteen, where I describe my arrival at the school, my "death row" march to the classroom, and my presentation to the students. The sub-points are:

- Arriving at school
- Walking into classroom
- Enduring the presentation

Finally, boxcar number three picks up at paragraph sixteen and takes the readers all the way through to paragraph twenty, covering the students' responses to my presentation and, in turn, my response to them. Here are the sub-points:

- Student speaks to me
- My response, initiating involvement from other students
- Further interaction with students

Paragraph twenty-one, of course, is the conclusion, or the caboose, of this train, ultimately resolving the conflict first introduced in the cow catcher and locomotive sections.

Now let's look at something a bit longer than our previous two examples. If your masterpiece happens to be a book rather than a short story or article, don't be overwhelmed or intimidated by the magnitude of your project. The train-of-thought writing method works for chapters within a book, just as it does for shorter manuscripts. Simply think of each chapter as a sort of sub-train within the main train, as well as one of the boxcars of the main train. As a "for instance," let's examine a very short chapter (a sub-train) from my still-in-progress novel *Emma Jean Reborn* (the main train), co-authored with Dr. Cupid Poe.

***

₁Emma Jean still couldn't believe she'd actually done it, though she hadn't been able to think of anything else since her visit from Sadie Garrett. It was as if Sadie had brought her a gift, a tiny sliver of hope that maybe—just maybe—there really was something better for her out there. All she'd had to do was figure out where "out there" was—and how to get there.

₂After a few days of thinking about it, she'd decided that "out there" must be California. She'd seen a couple of television programs about California when she and her parents had been visiting at the Johnson home, and she remembered thinking that it was always warm and sunny there. And the people in the TV programs were all so beautiful and rich, she just didn't see how anyone could be anything but happy in a place as wonderful as that.

₃And so she was on her way. Once the decision had been made, she'd waited for the first night that Gordon hadn't come home. Then she'd quickly stuffed a loaf of bread and what few personal clothes and belongings she had into an old pillowcase, grabbed the $47.23 that Gordon had stashed away in an old shoe in the back of the closet—a place Emma Jean was sure he imagined she'd never look—and then raced out the door and through the woods that paralleled the road out of town. Emma Jean had also seen a television program where a young man had hitchhiked across the country, but she knew she'd have to put a lot of miles between herself and Crooked River before she dared to stand out in plain view on the road, begging for a ride.

₄The first three days she'd stuck to the woods, making her way through the dense brush, eating her bread and drinking from the stream that meandered near her path. The nights were dark and cool, and she slept fitfully underneath the trees, snuggled up against her overstuffed pillowcase. One night she thought she heard Gordon calling her, but she lay very still, scarcely breathing, until the voice faded away. She never was sure if it had really been Gordon, or just a dream.

₅By the morning of the fourth day, long since she'd left behind any familiar territory, she got up the nerve to start walking along the road, cautiously turning and sticking out her thumb when an occasional car drove up behind her.

₆Her first ride had been with a large family. The parents and two youngest children rode inside the pickup's cab, and Emma Jean had been stuck in the back with the other five kids. When they first stopped and asked her where she was going, she'd told them California, and the parents had laughed. The children in the back, however, observed her wide-eyed, obviously impressed by her destination. Unfortunately the family took her only as far as the next town, which was about ten miles from where they'd picked her up. But at least she was able to find out where she was, and to figure out that she'd come almost fifty miles in her three-day journey. It was a lot farther than she'd ever gone in her life, but she knew it wasn't nearly far enough. There were many, many more miles to go, and she'd never make it walking.

₇After saying goodbye to the family, Emma Jean had stopped into a little store and bought some apples and cookies. Munching on a piece of fruit, she'd stuffed the rest of her newly purchased supplies into the pillowcase and headed back toward the road. She was going to have to find another ride, and she hoped it would be one that would take her more than just a few miles.

₈And that's how she'd met Jake. Not that he was the one to pick her up at first, though she certainly wished he had. Instead she'd found herself climbing into an old black Ford sedan that looked and sounded as if it were held together with chicken wire and road tar. But as they chugged down the road she'd told herself it didn't matter—as long as the overweight, middle-aged driver, who'd introduced himself as Billy, took her in the right direction. Billy had grinned at her when he'd stopped to offer her a ride and she'd asked how far he was going.

₉"Just up the road a piece," he'd answered, his grin widening as he spoke. "To my place. It ain't much, but it sits in the shade. Real cool, 'specially in the bedroom where the breeze blows right in the window."

10Emma Jean hadn't liked the sounds of that at all. "No thanks," she'd said, backing away from the car. "I need to go all the way to California. I'll just stick around and wait for somebody who's going a little farther."

11Billy's grin had faded. "Well, why didn't you say so?" he'd asked, reaching across the front seat and opening the passenger door. "Come on, get in. I'll take you to the truck stop up by the main highway. It's only 'bout twenty miles or so. You'll be able to catch a ride real easy there. Lotsa truckers headed all over the country. Bound to be one goin' to California that wouldn't mind takin' you along. Come on. Get in." When she still hesitated, he'd added, "Listen, you ain't gonna get a better offer than mine. Ain't many people 'round these parts gonna go outta their way to take somebody they don't even know all the way to the main highway."

12Emma Jean had thought about it for a moment, then decided he was probably right. So she'd slid into the passenger's seat and pulled the door shut, clutching her pillowcase in her left hand and keeping her right hand on the door handle—just in case. As it turned out, it was a smart move. They hadn't gone more than a couple of miles before Billy steered the old Ford onto a bumpy dirt driveway and into the woods.

13"Hey," Emma Jean had complained. "I thought you said you were taking me to the truck stop at the main highway."

14Billy kept driving. "Sure," he'd said, glancing over at her with a look that seemed to peel the clothes right off her body. "But first I'm gonna show you my place." His grin was back, slimier than ever. "You're gonna like it, I promise. Old Billy boy knows how to make his company feel real welcome."

15Emma Jean's heart thumped wildly as she yanked on the door handle and nearly catapulted herself from the slowly moving car. She hit the ground with a thud that momentarily winded her, but before Billy could stop the car and come after her, she was back on her feet and racing toward the road. She could hear the heavy man lumbering along behind her, but she was confident she could outrun him—and she did. But even as she turned and continued to run down the road, she realized her mistake. Billy had stopped chasing her, and no doubt had returned to his car. Old as the Ford was, she could never outrace it. She'd have to head back into the woods and hope her pursuer would decide it was too much trouble to pick his way through the brush and trees looking for her.

16Apparently her plan had worked, for she'd never seen or heard from old Billy again. But she'd had to give up hitchhiking and go back to trudging through the woods. Two days later she'd located the truck stop and plopped down at the counter to order her first real meal since leaving home. As she munched on her grilled cheese sandwich, her eyes darted around the room, checking out the dozen or so truckers at the place. Even if she could find one who was headed for California, how could she be sure he wasn't just another Billy? She was far too tired to have to run for her life again.

17Suddenly Sadie Garrett's words echoed in her mind. "All I know is that I was supposed to tell you he loves you and he has a plan for you, and he wants to help you. That's all." Was it possible, Emma Jean wondered. Had God really sent Sadie to deliver that message to her? It was, after all, the message that had given her the courage to finally leave Gordon Dawson and Crooked River behind. Maybe…

18*Are…are you there, God?* It was more a silent thought than a prayer, but Emma Jean decided that if there really was a God and he really did care for her, then he could hear her, even if she didn't speak out loud. *'Cause if you are, I really could use some of that help you promised….*

19Before she could think another word, a grizzled old man with a lined face and a crooked smile sat down next to her. Tufts of white hair stuck out from under a dirty old baseball cap, and his left hand was withered. But his pale blue eyes were warm, and she felt at ease with him immediately.

20"Where ya headed, missy?" he asked, his voice gravelly with age.

21"California."

22The old man raised his bushy eyebrows. "California?" He smiled his crooked smile, and Emma Jean noticed that some of his teeth were missing. "Now why'd I know you'd say that?" He shook his head. "God sure is full of surprises, ain't he?"

23Now it was Emma Jean's turn to raise her eyebrows. "God?"

24The old man nodded. "Yep. Hadn't even planned to stop in here today, but felt like I should. And here you are, headed for California, just like me." He hesitated before introducing himself. "My name's Jake. And you're...?"

25Emma Jean swallowed before answering. "I'm...Emma Jean." She was glad Jake hadn't given her his last name. That way she didn't feel obliged to tell him hers—either Cooper or Dawson. She just wanted to leave that part of her identity behind and hope that maybe she just might find Emma Jean in the process.

26Jake smiled again. "So, you need a ride? 'Cause I'm just about ready to head out, and I sure could use some company."

27Emma Jean swallowed and nodded, amazed that she felt no hesitation in accepting the old man's offer. She reached into her pocket for some money to pay her bill, but Jake shook his head and laid his good hand on her arm. "It's on me," he said, dropping a couple of dollar bills on the counter. "Come on. Let's go. We got a long trip ahead of us."

28And that's how Emma Jean had found herself sitting in the cab of Jake's diesel truck, barreling down the highway toward California, amazed at how fast her life seemed to be changing. It had been less than two weeks since Sadie had come to visit her that night, and now she was on her way. She could hardly wait to see what would happen once she arrived at her destination.

***

The cow catcher in this chapter is extremely brief: "Emma Jean still couldn't believe she'd actually done it." Done what? Whatever it was, readers know it must have been something rather startling because Emma Jean can scarcely believe she has done it. The readers will therefore be anxious to continue on in the journey. The remainder of that first paragraph completes the locomotive, explaining to the readers that what Emma Jean just did had something to do with a visit from someone named Sadie Garrett. (Readers of the book have just read about that visit in the previous chapter, so they're now clued in to where this chapter is going.)

The first boxcar in this example begins in paragraph two and continues into paragraph three, describing what it was that Emma Jean actually did, as we see in the boxcar's sub-points:

- Thought about what to do
- Decided to go to California
- Waited until Gordon was gone
- Took a few personal belongings and a little money
- Ran off through the woods

The second boxcar is contained in paragraph four, which tells of Emma Jean's first days on the run:

- Stuck to the woods

- Stayed close to the stream

- Slept beneath trees

- Thought she heard Gordon calling her

Boxcar number three begins in paragraph five and continues through paragraph seven, telling of her first ride:

- Ventures out of the woods on fourth day

- Hitches a ride with a family

- Ten miles later family drops her off in town

- Discovers she'd traveled fifty miles before meeting up with the family

- Buys supplies and hits the road to look for another ride

The fourth boxcar is a bit longer, extending from paragraph eight through fifteen and revealing her meeting with a man named Billy.

- Description of Billy's vehicle and their initial meeting

- Billy's offer to take her to his place, and her refusal

- Billy's offer to drive her to a truck stop by the main highway

- Emma Jean's continued hesitation but final acceptance

- Billy's ulterior motive becomes apparent

- Emma Jean escapes from the car and runs from Billy

The fifth boxcar takes place upon Emma Jean's arrival at the truck stop, and covers paragraphs sixteen through eighteen.

- Two days after escaping from Billy she arrives at the truck stop

- Orders a sandwich and wonders what to do next

- Remembers Sadie's words

- Prays, asking God for help

The final boxcar describes her meeting with Jake; it begins in paragraph nineteen and continues through paragraph twenty-seven.

- Old man sits down next to her
- She feels comfortable with him
- They talk and find out they're both headed to California
- They introduce themselves by first names only
- Jake offers her a ride
- Emma Jean accepts
- Jake pays for her meal as they prepare to leave

The final paragraph is the caboose for this novel's chapter (the sub-train within the main train), tying together the sub-points of the six boxcars and also serving as a "coupler," or transition, to the next chapter in the novel. (We will discuss couplers in detail in our next chapter.)

With these three examples as your guidelines, it's time to start construction of the main part of your own train, though at this point your primary focus is to identify your boxcars and attempt to put them into a logical sequence. Working with a partner on this aspect of your boxcar construction is beneficial, and I encourage you to do so. However, as I said before, once your boxcars are labeled and in order and you're ready to start the actual writing, you'll probably discover that it's easier to work alone. You can always get back together afterward to critique your partner's work.

One more note at this crucial juncture: Although each section of your train is equally important, this is the section that will consume the most of your time, so be patient with yourself—and with your partner, if you have one. Even a short article or story deserves all the time necessary to get it done right. So whether you are working on a short story or a book-length manuscript, take as long as you need in constructing your boxcars.

Chapter Five

"The Couplers"

My husband and I once went to visit our beloved Uncle Arnold (on my husband's side) when he was in the hospital in downtown Los Angeles. As the day wore on we got hungry and invited Aunt Carmen, Arnold's wife, to go out to dinner with us. We didn't know the area very well so we asked at the hospital's information desk about a good place to eat. They recommended a nearby restaurant and said we couldn't miss it because it was in a railroad-car-turned-diner. Sure enough, we had no trouble finding it, and the three of us enjoyed an excellent meal together. (We left poor Uncle Arnold behind to eat hospital food, but thankfully he made a full recovery in spite of it.)

However, as much as we enjoyed our meal and our visit with Aunt Carmen, we never expected that railroad car to start chugging away and take us on a trip while we ate. We knew our dining car was stationary for several reasons:

- It was not sitting on a railroad track
- There was no locomotive anywhere in sight
- It was not connected to any other railroad car

Sound ridiculous? All right, maybe the example is a no-brainer. But even if our dining car had been sitting on a track at the train station, in line behind a locomotive and other railroad cars, it would never have moved if it weren't connected to those other cars.

The same is true in writing. You may have several well-built boxcars, all aligned in perfect order, but if they're disconnected from each other, they will never move your readers along on your word journey. Let's look again at one of the examples from the previous chapter on boxcars, only this time without the couplers.

***

1"Paper or plastic, ma'am?"

2It doesn't seem that long ago when my mother was teaching me to respect my elders—and now I am one!

3Even though the term "ma'am" is meant to convey respect, it's hard to keep that in mind when hearing it makes you feel as old as Methuselah.

4It isn't that I'm as old as the people I used to refer to as "ma'am" and "sir"; it's that people are now being born at a much younger age.

5When was the last time you checked out the age of a fireman or a policeman or an ambulance driver? Surely they don't allow them to participate in these professions before the age of fourteen, and yet none of the ones I've seen lately looked old enough to shave.

6 & 7My elderly neighbor was once pulled over for driving too slowly. "I told that young whippersnapper I didn't need any advice from him," she explained. "After all, I was driving before he was born."

8He let her go with only a warning—which she ignored completely.

9They're graduating those guys from the police academy younger and younger all the time. (I wonder if that's why some of them ride bikes instead of driving cars—they're simply not old enough to get a driver's license.)

10Some doctors look like they just blew in from an after-school sock hop, and braces on surgeons do not inspire confidence.

11We baby boomers should be careful not to get sucked into a youth-oriented world or we'll waste the best years of our lives reminiscing about the "good old days."

12What was so good about being young? Would you really want to be a teenager again? (I'd rather eat cat food.) Besides, it only takes about ten years to get used to how old you are, so be patient.

13English poet Robert Browning wrote these famous lines:

Grow old along with me! The best is yet to be

The last of life, for which the first was made;

Our times are in His hand.

14It doesn't hurt so much to be called "ma'am." In fact, I think I kind of like it!

***

Now, because you've already read the complete article, including the couplers, it probably wasn't too difficult to follow along with this abbreviated version. But if you were to read this version first, it might not be such a smooth read. Let's compare the two versions, paragraph by paragraph, stressing the couplers between each paragraph rather than just between the individual boxcars, so you can get a clearer picture of the need for smooth transitions all the way through.

First, let's look at the opening three paragraphs in the revised version, the one without the couplers. "Paper or plastic, ma'am?" is still the cow catcher, but there is nothing to tie it naturally or smoothly to the next two paragraphs, which make up the locomotive. Readers may be able to conclude, after reading these three paragraphs, that this is probably going to be a piece about my struggle with aging, but their own struggle with reading such a disconnected story may preclude their ever finishing it.

In the original piece I stressed the word "ma'am" three times in the opening paragraph in order to cement it in the readers' minds. I then opened paragraph two with "Do you know what a shock it is the first time you realize...," which clearly tells the readers that I was personally shocked the first time I was referred to as "ma'am." Now it's evident that this is not only a story on aging in general, but also that it's a personal experience story about aging. Because the stress on the word "ma'am" in the first paragraph, along with the opening sentence in the second paragraph, are omitted in the second version of this piece, the natural transition, or coupler, is missing. Already the story has lost its flow. In essence, the readers are beginning to sense that the journey is going nowhere fast.

Moving from paragraph two to paragraph three in the second version confirms the readers' suspicions that this is going to be a disjointed trip, as once again there is no smooth transition from one paragraph to the next. In the original version I drew the readers in by opening the third paragraph with a question: "It's a strange feeling, isn't it?" Now the readers are identifying with my feelings, and instead of simply reading what I've written, the readers and I are having a conversation. Without that coupler to move the readers to paragraph three, all they get is another statement about how old I'm feeling.

The same is true when we move from paragraph three to paragraph four. The coupler here—"But I have a theory"—piques the readers' curiosity and makes the prospective journey more appealing. The next coupler—"Think about it"—opens paragraph five and is a personal invitation to the readers to stay onboard. "I used to laugh at my elderly neighbor's story..." opens the next paragraph and introduces some emotion into the piece, keeping the journey alive. The omission of that particular coupler in the revised version made it necessary to combine what remained of the original paragraphs six and seven, making that story about my neighbor much less personal and humorous. Then, by leaving out the coupler at the beginning of paragraph eight of the original piece ("He must have been impressed with her logic"), we miss the assumed reason that the policeman let my neighbor go without writing her a ticket.

Okay, let's look at the opening sentence of paragraph nine in the original version: "But now I'm beginning to think maybe she was right." This is a strong coupler, pulling the readers from the story about my neighbor back to me and my own thoughts on aging. Without that sentence the readers wonder at my comments in the revised version of paragraph nine. When I say, "They're graduating those guys from the police academy younger and younger all the time," am I specifically referring to the officer who pulled my neighbor over, or to policemen in general? The inclusion of the coupler clarifies that point.

The opening sentence in the original paragraph ten is a strong coupler that pulls us from the topic of young policemen to young doctors: "The worst thing, however, is when you go to the doctor and he looks like he just blew in from an after-school sock hop." This transition from policemen to doctors is missing entirely in the opening sentence of the revised paragraph ten: "Some doctors look like they just blew in from an after-school sock hop." Though my readers will eventually figure out that I've moved from policemen to doctors, they may also wonder if it's worth the effort to continue this journey any longer.

The opening sentence in the original paragraph eleven is another conversational point between me and my readers: "Let's face it." Translation? We're in this together, which is confirmed in the first word of the next sentence, "we." Then, in the original paragraph twelve, I open with a coupler that is a challenge to the readers: "Be truthful." Again, the readers' curiosity is piqued. Be truthful about what? This flows easily into the questions, "What was so good about being young? Would you really want to be a teenager again?" Though I open the revised paragraph twelve with those two questions, the readers miss the personal challenge ("Be truthful") that pulls them from the mention of the "good old days," which are the last words in paragraph eleven, to the questions of paragraph twelve. Then the coupler between the original paragraphs twelve and thirteen—"Personally I'm inclined to agree with the English poet Robert Browning"—keeps the piece on a personal level and helps bring the readers along from the points in paragraph twelve to the poem in paragraph thirteen.

Finally, the coupler between the poem in the original paragraph thirteen and the caboose in paragraph fourteen—"With that in mind"—helps bring the readers to a natural conclusion to the entire piece and a feeling that the ride has come to a satisfying end (a topic we will discuss in detail in the final chapter of this book).

And that's what couplers do: They help keep the readers on board for a smooth and satisfying journey. In fact, Webster's definition of a coupler is "a person or thing that couples; specif., *a)* a device for coupling two railroad cars *b)* a device on an organ connecting two keyboards or keys an octave apart *so that they can be played together*" (emphasis added). Isn't that interesting? We see in this definition a reference to railroad cars being held together, but also to music—"two keyboards or keys an octave apart so that they can be played together." What an easy and natural transition it would be from music to writing if we defined a coupler as "a device connecting two paragraphs or words/sentences in paragraphs so they can be read with the same focus."

All right, are you ready for some exercises in writing couplers? I'll give you two sets of two paragraphs each; your job is to write a coupler to link the two paragraphs in each set together. (This is a great time to get with your partner, as there is more brainstorming than actual writing in these two exercises.)

***

    The gathering clouds should have been a warning to Janet, but she scarcely noticed them. Even the gusts of icy wind that whipped her long hair into her eyes didn't seem to faze her.

    Claudia shook her head and sighed. What else was there to do? Hadn't she already tried everything possible to prevent this senseless tragedy? Besides, regardless of her actions at this point, nothing good could ever come of such a depressing and macabre situation.

***

These paragraphs could be the opening to a short story or a novel, or even a non-fiction piece. The all-important cow catcher is obvious in the first sentence, but after that things seem to break down. Though the second sentence builds on the first, we then find ourselves jolted from paragraph one to paragraph two, as we shift from Janet's story to Claudia's. Is there a connection between the two women? Is Claudia's dilemma related to Janet's situation? Are they aware of one another? What can the readers possibly conclude at this point?

It is obvious we need a transition between the two paragraphs—and that is your assignment. On the spaces below (after brainstorming alone or with your partner), construct a coupler (use only as many sentences as are absolutely necessary) that will help the readers begin to understand the connection (if any) between Janet and Claudia, as well as a "feel" for where this word journey will take them.

_____

_____

_____

_____

_____

_____

Here is a brief sample transition that I wrote for this exercise, but keep in mind that mine is no more "right" than yours. It is simply an example to help you examine your own coupler. (The coupler is highlighted in bold-face print.)

***

The gathering clouds should have been a warning to Janet, but she scarcely noticed them. Even the gusts of icy wind that whipped her long hair into her eyes didn't seem to faze her. **Emily was gone, and nothing could bring her back now, though she knew Claudia had tried to stop her from leaving. Claudia always tried; that's just the type of person she was. *The good one. Not like me…*. Even now Janet knew that Claudia was watching her, but she just couldn't bring herself to turn and acknowledge her older sister.**

Claudia shook her head and sighed. What else was there to do? Hadn't she already tried everything possible to prevent this senseless tragedy? Besides, regardless of her actions at this point, nothing good could ever come of such a depressing and macabre situation.

***

With my coupler inserted at the end of paragraph one, the readers can more easily make the transition from Janet to Claudia, knowing that they're sisters and that they're involved in the same situation. The readers also know that the two women are close enough to see one another, and that Claudia had tried to prevent some sort of tragedy that somehow related to someone named Emily. Though there are still a lot of details to unfold, the readers now have enough information to be curious about the outcome, while not being confused by the scenario.

All right, let's look at one more example before you try writing the couplers for your own boxcars.

***

The year-round weather in Kona (often called the "Gold Coast") is just about as perfect as it gets. The lifestyle is several paces slower and much more relaxing than on the Mainland, though the cost of living is a bit higher. In addition, because Kona is located on Hawaii, or the "Big Island," residents are less likely to experience island fever than are residents of the smaller islands that make up America's fiftieth state.

Our retirement years are quickly approaching. For most of us a set income dictates, at least in part, where we will live out those golden years, as do other practical issues, such as proximity to family and friends. Ultimately, however, beauty and tranquility beckon, and we are prone to follow our heart.

***

These two brief paragraphs could easily be found at the beginning or even in the middle of an article about Hawaii, travel in general, or retirement choices. Yet whatever the topic or wherever the placement in the piece, the first paragraph simply does not flow well into the second. Readers are left to assume that the writer is referring to Kona as a possible retirement destination, but even that assumption is shaky. For our second exercise in creating couplers, use the lines below (either alone or with your partner) to write a brief coupler that will tie the two paragraphs together and make the meaning clearer to the readers.

_____

_____

_____

_____

_____

_____

How did you do? Did this one flow more easily than the last? Here is my suggestion for pulling the paragraphs together with a coupler. (Again, my coupler is highlighted with bold-face type.)

***

The year-round weather in Kona (often called the "Gold Coast") is just about as perfect as it gets. The lifestyle is several paces slower and much more relaxing than on the Mainland, though the cost of living is a bit higher. In addition, because Kona is located on Hawaii, or the "Big Island," residents are less likely to experience island fever than are residents of the smaller islands that make up America's fiftieth state.

Personally, my husband and I can't imagine ever experiencing island fever in any part of Hawaii, let alone Kona, which is our hands-down favorite spot on earth. Though we never before dreamed we would one day live there, we now find ourselves seriously considering it, as our retirement years are quickly approaching. For most of us a set income dictates, at least in part, where we will live out those golden years, as do other practical issues, such as proximity to family and friends. Ultimately, however, beauty and tranquility beckon, and we are prone to follow our heart.

***

This time I have placed my coupler at the beginning of the second paragraph, rather than at the end of the first. As you can see I haven't added much, but enough to help pull readers from the first paragraph into the second, making the transition from talking about Kona in general to Kona as a possible retirement spot much more personal and specific. The readers now have a relatively clear idea where this journey will take them.

One more note about couplers before we return to the construction of your own masterpiece: There are times in a manuscript, particularly a novel, when you simply have to skip ahead in time. This is where a smooth transition is vital. You need to bring your readers along quickly without making them feel they missed something. As an example, let's look again at the opening paragraphs from the chapter I pulled from my novel *Emma Jean Reborn*, an excerpt you read in the chapter on boxcars.

***

1Emma Jean still couldn't believe she'd actually done it, though she hadn't been able to think of anything else since her visit from Sadie Garrett. It was as if Sadie had brought her a gift, a tiny sliver of hope that maybe—just maybe—there really was something better for her out there. All she'd had to do was figure out where "out there" was—and how to get there.

2After a few days of thinking about it, she'd decided that "out there" must be California. She'd seen a couple of television programs about California when she and her parents had been visiting at the Johnson home, and she remembered thinking that it was always warm and sunny there. And the people in the TV programs were all so beautiful and rich, she just didn't see how anyone could be anything but happy in a place as wonderful as that.

3**And so she was on her way.** Once the decision had been made, she'd waited for the first night that Gordon hadn't come home. Then she'd quickly stuffed a loaf of bread and what few personal clothes and belongings she had into an old pillowcase, grabbed the $47.23 that Gordon had stashed away in an old shoe in the back of the closet—a place Emma Jean was sure he imagined she'd never look—and then raced out the door and through the woods that paralleled the road out of town. Emma Jean had also seen a television program where a young man had hitchhiked across the country, but she knew she'd have to put a lot of miles between herself and Crooked River before she dared to stand out in plain view on the road, begging for a ride.

***

Do you see how I covered several days in just a few short paragraphs? The highlighted, opening sentence in paragraph three—"And so she was on her way"—is the coupler or transition that moves the readers from the time of Emma Jean's planning to leave home to the actual trip itself. This enabled me to set the scene during her journey, which is a major focus of the book, while not leaving the readers wondering how she finally got the nerve and the wherewithal to make the break. And it was accomplished without including any unnecessary detail.

Okay, now it's time for you to work on your own transitions. Again, this is the time you can brainstorm with a partner and later compare notes, but the actual construction of your couplers will probably be easier if done alone on your computer, word processor, or typewriter. You may find, as you work through your existing boxcars, that you don't need a coupler or transition between each set of paragraphs, as some may already flow quite nicely. But pay close attention to the transition points between the actual boxcars and sub-points, as you want to be certain that you don't leave any part of your train disconnected from the rest. Then, when you've finished creating your couplers, we'll be ready to move on to the observation car, which will teach us how to breathe life into our train of words.

Chapter Six

"The Observation Car"

The 2005 film titled "Are We There Yet?" is supposed to be a comedy, but as a parent and grandparent who has heard that infamous "Are we there yet?" question a gazillion times, I can easily relate to the frustrated adult who is driving those squabbling, pint-sized terrorists across the country.

"He touched me!"

"Did not!"

"Did too!"

"That's because she was looking at me!"

"Was not!"

"Were too!"

"See? He's doing it again."

"Am not. And stop putting your leg over on my side!"

Sound familiar? It does if you've ever ridden in a car with passengers under the age of thirteen. (Once they're teenagers it gets worse!) But what, other than the obvious sibling rivalry, causes such annoying behavior? Personally, I think it's boredom, plain and simple. Kids do not want to spend a lot of time confined in a car, whether they're going to Disneyland or the dentist. They just want to get there.

Readers are much the same way. If they find themselves on a long, boring ride, they want one of two things: to get off at the next stop, or to get to their destination as quickly as possible. And to be truthful, it doesn't matter how expertly we've aligned our boxcars or how smooth a ride the perfectly constructed couplers are providing. If the ride is boring, the readers just want out. Therefore, to prevent mass defection, we must make sure our journey doesn't get boring.

So how do we do that? We add an observation car, an element that will breathe life into our word train and enable our readers to get caught up in their journey to the point that they will no longer be concerned about whether or not they're "there yet"; they will care only about what they'll discover around the next bend.

If you've ever ridden on a train you know that all the passenger cars have windows, and if you have a window seat you can see outside. But your view from these cars is limited. The observation car is different. It is specifically designed to enable passengers to see as much scenery as possible, with glass on both sides and even overhead, and with the seats arranged so that everyone in the car gets a great view.

Suddenly the long, boring ride is much more entertaining. Why? Because the passengers can see what's going on—in front of them, beside them, above them, and behind them. Without these added dimensions, the ride quickly becomes flat and unappealing. The same is true of our writing, regardless of our destination. What good is breathtaking scenery if no one can see it?

Imagine taking a train ride in a passenger car with no windows. The conductor stands at the front of the car, reciting from memory the passing scenery over a loudspeaker. The passengers may accept the fact that they're riding through the redwoods because that's what the conductor is telling them, but how much more effective would it be if they could actually see the majestic giants?

That's the difference between show and tell. Would you prefer that someone *tell* you there are trees outside, or would you rather have someone open a window and *show* them to you? The age-old writer's maxim of "show, don't tell" is good, solid advice, but simply sprinkling your work with a few more adjectives and adverbs is not the way to accomplish it.

For instance, if I tell you there are trees outside, you may visualize tall trees, short trees, evergreens, palm trees, barren trees, etc. If I tell you there are large, straight, green, leaf-laden trees outside, you have a clearer picture through the added use of adjectives, but you still don't know if the trees are fragile-leafed aspens dancing in the wind or sturdy oaks with shade-bearing limbs. And that's the key. "Fragile-leafed aspens dancing in the wind" paints a clear picture in our mind. It *shows* us what type of tree is outside, as does the phrase "sturdy oaks with shade-bearing limbs." The secret is not to load up your writing with more and more adjectives, but rather to add better adjectives and/or stronger nouns. For example, just as the words *fragile* and *sturdy* are strong adjectives, *aspens* and *oaks* are strong nouns.

The same is true of verbs and adverbs. Instead of *telling* our readers that "Jane ran quickly down the road," we *show* them the action by saying, "Jane raced down the road." Rather than *telling* readers how "Mark hurriedly made his way past the entrance," we *show* them by saying "Mark scurried past the entrance." Do you see the difference? One strong verb (*raced* or *scurried*) is always preferable to a weak verb supported by one or more adverbs (*ran quickly* or *hurriedly made his way*).

The most important aspect of the observation car, however, is not the scenery as much as it is the people. If you're riding along in a train's observation car, sooner or later you're going to get tired of doing nothing but staring out the window, and you're going to start throwing spit-wads at the guy next to you and yelling, "Are we there yet?" Regardless of your age or how majestic those redwoods are, if you've seen a couple hundred of them, you've seen enough! But observing the other passengers…well, that's another story.

Think about it. Have you ever been stuck in an airport and had to find a way to kill some time until your flight was called? What did you do? Buy a ten-dollar bag of chips at an overpriced cafeteria? Read a book? Open your laptop and jot down a few lines? Play a game or two of solitaire? Maybe. But eventually you were distracted by the many people coming and going around you, and you found yourself caught up in the mini-dramas—real or imagined—of their lives.

People-watching is contagious. We all do it, and we do it for one reason: People, for the most part, are interesting. Short ones, stout ones, tall ones, slim ones, black ones, white ones, old ones, young ones…it doesn't matter. Each one has a story, and it's just waiting to be told. Readers sense this, whether they're conscious of it or not. A solo train ride is lonely and dull. Bring in a few colorful characters, and the journey takes on an entirely new perspective.

So how do you do it? How do you enable your readers to sit in the observation car of your word train and visualize not only the passing scenery but also the interesting and exciting passengers that populate your manuscript? Well, first you must know these people yourself. Have you ever tried to describe someone you didn't know? Not an easy task, is it? But the more time you spend with a character and the more knowledgeable you become about the intimate details of that person's life, the more accurate and fascinating a portrait you will paint for your readers.

Now I know that some of you may be thinking, *Wait a minute! This people thing might work for fiction, but I'm writing nonfiction. Why do I need to put people in my article/book?* For the exact reason I mentioned above: to keep it from being boring.

More than once I have been hired to work with a nonfiction author for the express purpose of breathing life into a promising but lackluster manuscript. The facts and figures were all there; the material was well organized, documented, and presented; even the author's name gave the manuscript credibility. But the average reader wouldn't have made it through the first chapter without dying of boredom.

My job was to write an introduction to each chapter, a human illustration to lay the groundwork for what was to come. In other words, through the use of "people situations" (either real or imagined), I *showed* the readers what the author was about to *tell* them. My illustrations were brief and to the point, but the people in my illustrations had to be memorable enough to make an impression on the readers. Of course, these people examples don't have to be confined to the beginning of a book chapter or an article; they can be placed anywhere throughout the piece where they would be effective in illustrating a specific point. And that's where our observation car comes into play.

Whether writing fiction or nonfiction, your characters must be three-dimensional; that doesn't happen simply by giving them blond hair and blue eyes, or broad shoulders and dazzling smiles. Before I begin a novel, I create my main characters. This means I detail these characters in such a way that I would immediately recognize them if I saw them walking down the street—which is exactly the way I want my readers to feel about them.

Following is a suggested format for creating a believable character. If you're writing nonfiction you probably won't need to fill in all the blanks, but the more you do, the stronger your people examples will be. As you work through the list you'll probably wonder why you would need to know certain things about your characters, such as favorite music or food, if you don't plan to mention those specific points in your piece. However, the more you know about your characters, the more accurately you will be able to portray their habits, motives, dreams, and goals to your readers.

All right, let's give it a try. Even if you don't have a particular character in mind for your manuscript at this point, see if you can develop one as a sort of model for future works. (I think you'll find this exercise to be a lot of fun, particularly if you're working with a partner.)

Name/nickname: _____

Age/birthdate: _____

Physical description: _____

_____

_____

_____

Birthplace and current place of residence: _____

_____

Family situation/members: _____

_____

_____

_____

Friends/best friend/romantic interest: _____

_____

_____

Education: _____

Occupation: _____

Hobbies/outside interests: _____

_____

_____

_____

Quirks/eccentricities: _____

_____

_____

_____

Strong points/weak points: _____

_____

_____

_____

Favorite song/type of music/TV program/movie: _____

_____

_____

_____

Favorite book(s)/magazine(s) _____

_____

_____

Favorite food(s)/restaurant(s): _____

_____

_____

_____

Favorite type of architecture/furnishings/décor: _____

_____

_____

_____

Contents of medicine cabinet: _____

_____

_____

_____

Contents of purse/wallet/car's glove compartment: _____

_____

_____

_____

Favorite/least favorite ways to travel: _____

_____

_____

Favorite car (same as or different from type owned?): _____

_____

_____

Favorite sport(s), if any (fan only, or also a participant?): _____

_____

_____

_____

Way of speaking (proper/accent/slang/pet words or phrases?): _____

_____

_____

_____

Personality/temperament: _____

_____

_____

_____

Reputation (earned or otherwise): _____

_____

_____

_____

Reaction to crises/insults/threats/good or bad news: _____

_____

_____

_____

Skeletons in closet: _____

_____

_____

_____

Dreams/aspirations/goals: _____

_____

_____

Fears/phobias/obsessions: _____

_____

_____

_____

Pets:_____

_____

_____

Spiritual life/faith/political leanings/worldview: _____

_____

_____

_____

Although there certainly is much more that can be added to any character's data, this should be enough to give you a clear picture of the person you're trying to describe to your readers. Admittedly it takes time to fill out so much information for each character in your manuscript, and you probably won't need to include every bit of the above information when writing about your characters. But the more you know about them, the better you can picture them in your mind and judge how they might react in any given situation—which, of course, is what makes them true-to-life.

And that's how you create three-dimensional characters who will make your train's observation car the highlight of your word journey, and also diminish your chances of hearing your readers whine, "Are we there yet?"

Chapter Seven

"The Caboose"

All good things must come to an end. Ever hear that statement? Of course you have. But let's look at it carefully and see what we can learn from it in relation to our word train.

The two key words here are "good" and "must." All *good* things *must* come to an end. This implies that when we're enjoying something we don't particularly want to see it end. However, if this positive assertion is true, can we also assume that there are some *not-so-good* things that might never come to an end? Or does it just seem that way when we're in the midst of enduring one of those not-so-good things—such as poor writing?

When I'm reading a good novel I can't wait to get to the end so I can see how the story turns out. At the same time, I really don't want the story to end because I'm enjoying it so much. In this case, our statement of "all good things must come to an end" certainly seems to apply. But if I'm plodding my way through a dismally boring, disjointed, poorly written manuscript, it doesn't take long before I find myself wondering if it will ever end. (Sound familiar—as in, "Are we there yet?")

The only thing worse than being forced to read all the way through a bad piece of writing is to read through a good piece and find it has a bad ending—or no ending at all. A properly constructed word train must be complemented by a strong and satisfying caboose. The ending of a manuscript should tie together everything that has gone before, much the same way that a caboose signals the end of a passing train.

For instance, have you ever watched an old movie where the hero and heroine are disappearing into the sunset on a train? Where do they stand to wave goodbye—on the locomotive, a boxcar, the observation car? Of course not. They stand at the railing at the very back of the caboose—the last part of the train—symbolically signaling the end of the story with a wave. If you enjoyed the movie, you may regret seeing that final wave, but you recognize that the story is over, and you're satisfied with the ending.

That's how we must leave our readers when they come to the end of our manuscript—perhaps a bit nostalgic, but definitely satisfied. What could be worse than reading the last line of a story and then turning the page, expecting more but finding nothing, feeling frustrated that the story had suddenly stopped, rather than ended? There is a great difference between the two, and if we simply stop writing rather than end our stories satisfactorily, we do a great disservice to our readers and seriously damage our reputation as writers.

One of the common complaints I've heard about newspaper writing is that articles suddenly seem to stop, as if the writer ran out of space. Guess what? In most cases, that's exactly what happened. Newspaper writing is quite different from book or article writing. Newspaper writers learn to squeeze all the major facts—who, what, where, when, why, and how—into the first few paragraphs of an article because they never know if the last few paragraphs of their piece might get cut for space. But that's not the case in the types of word journeys we're discussing in this book, so we have no excuse for stopping our work, rather than ending it.

Let's look at a few sample endings and see if we can get a clearer picture of what it means to complete our train with a strong caboose. The first two examples are from books one and seven of *The Chronicles of Narnia*, a seven-story fiction series written by one of my favorite authors, C. S. Lewis. Though these classic books are often viewed as having been written for children, I still enjoy reading them as a grandmother—whether my grandchildren are around to listen or not! If you've never experienced this wonderful series, I hope you'll be anxious to do so once you've seen how expertly this author draws these two books to a close.

***

Book One: *The Magician's Nephew*

(**Summary**: This opening book of the series tells the story of two friends who are instantly transported into another world called Narnia, where an evil sorceress seeks to enslave them. But then the Great Lion, Aslan, is introduced into the children's adventure, and suddenly anything seems possible.)

Ending: When Digory and his people went to live in the big country house, they took Uncle Andrew to live with them; for Digory's father said, "We must try to keep the old fellow out of mischief, and it isn't fair that poor Letty should have him always on her hands." Uncle Andrew never tried any Magic again as long as he lived. He had learned his lesson, and in his old age he became a nicer and less selfish old man than he had ever been before. But he always liked to get visitors alone in the billiard-room and tell them stories about a mysterious lady, a foreign royalty, with whom he had driven about London. "A devilish temper she had," he would say. "But she was a dem fine woman, sir, a dem fine woman."

Book Seven: *The Last Battle*

(**Summary**: This final book of the series takes place during the last days of Narnia, when the land faces its fiercest challenge from an enemy within. Only the king and his band of loyal followers can stop the total destruction of all they hold dear.)

Ending: And as He spoke He no longer looked to them like a lion; but the things that began to happen after that were so great and beautiful that I cannot write them. And for us this is the end of all the stories, and we can most truly say that they all lived happily ever after. But for them it was only the beginning of the real story. All their life in this world and all their adventures in Narnia had only been the cover and the title page: now at last they were beginning Chapter One of the Great Story which no one on earth has read: which goes on forever: in which every chapter is better than the one before.

***

Not only are these books classics, but so are their endings. Many might say the endings' happily-ever-after tone is unrealistic and outdated, and in today's literary world that may be so. However, we need to remember that these decades-old allegorical books of fantasy were written primarily for children, and children like happily-ever-after endings. (So do I!)

Now, unless you've already read the books, you don't have the advantage of knowing who Digory and Uncle Andrew and Letty are. But even without that knowledge, you can read these endings and know that the author has constructed some fine cabooses for the end of his trains. In the ending to the first book, *The Magician's Nephew* (as is true of books two through six), the ending is a satisfying close to the story contained in that book but it doesn't preclude another story picking up where that one left off. In fact, it leaves readers hoping for exactly that. In the ending to the final book, however (where even the title of *The Last Battle* is effective in indicating the end of the series), we see the "last caboose" neatly tying together all the loose ends of the story contained within that book, as well as all the loose ends of the series itself. This final ending is hopeful and positive, though a bit of a sad farewell, and the readers have no doubt that they've come to the end of their journey through Narnia.

Now let's look at a couple of nonfiction examples from a much less prominent writer. The first is an interview I did for a newspaper nearly twenty years ago. At that time the small town where I lived was experiencing unprecedented growth, and many of the mom-and-pop stores were being driven out of business by the large department stores that were moving into the area. My assignment was to interview a family whose hardware store had served the community for sixty years; my goal was to point out to the newspaper's readers the advantages of coming to a store where the owners were an established part of the community. After talking about how the store was started in 1926 and passed from the original generation of owners to the next, I wove in some of the town's history, much of which was unknown to many of the newly transplanted residents. Then I discussed the upcoming anniversary celebration before ending with these three simple paragraphs that constituted my caboose.

***

What plans are there for the future of Whitaker Hardware? According to James, although there are plans to "readjust the inventory to fit the needs of a growing and changing community," they expect things to remain pretty much as they were in the days when they sold horse collars and buggy whips.

"Personal service," James and Sylvia agree. "Treating our customers as friends. That's the tradition we want to see carried on."

And it will be. That's what Whitaker Hardware is all about.

***

Not exactly a Pulitzer Prize-winning piece of journalism, but a heartwarming story about the ongoing generations of a family who dedicated themselves to the needs of the community in which they lived. That was the focus of the story, the tracks on which I built my entire word train, and that's what I stressed as I brought the piece to a close. (Fortunately it was a front-page feature so my caboose wasn't cut for space.)

Now let's look at another example, comparing a story that just stops to the same story with a satisfying ending. Do you remember the excerpt you read in the boxcars chapter, taken from my novel *Emma Jean Reborn*? The book deals with the life of a young girl born into poverty and raised on racism and abuse, who finally escapes and goes out on her own in an effort to find a better life. With that in mind, here is one way I could have "stopped" the book, leaving the readers frustrated and dissatisfied with the outcome.

***

Now that Emma Jean was back home in Crooked River she decided it was time to get a job and get on with her life. She'd been feeling sorry for herself long enough, and she hoped something better was finally on the horizon.

***

Even without having read the entire story, you can see that this is a flat ending. Though our caboose has the basic facts, it doesn't tie them together or present them in such a way that the readers feel their journey has been successfully completed. Let's look now at the way I really ended the story and see if it leaves you feeling much more satisfied with the outcome.

***

As she sat in her car and watched the first drops of rain begin to splatter on the windshield, she thought of the precious old book she'd carried around with her now for so many years. Looking down at it on the front seat beside her, she stroked its cover.

"Forgiveness works," she whispered, and then, after a few seconds, she started her car and backed out of the parking space. Suddenly it didn't matter how the test came out. Emma Jean knew she couldn't fail because she was no longer a victim. Turning onto the street that headed toward home, she began to sing along with the music. Life was good, and she was going to be all right.

***

This isn't a classic happily-ever-after ending where we know for certain that absolutely everything is going to go well for Emma Jean from here on out; it is, however, a positive and hopeful ending, leaving readers with the feeling that Emma Jean has come of age and moved past the tragedy of her past. Readers are now confident that Emma Jean is indeed going to be all right. And since that was the primary concern throughout the book, the loose ends have now been tied together and the caboose has done its job.

Now it's your turn to work on creating your own caboose. This is a point where I would challenge you first to get together with your partner, assuming you've been working with one all along, and once again begin to brainstorm. Ask each other the following questions concerning one another's manuscripts, and then write your answers on the lines provided.

Have I stayed "on track" throughout the manuscript? _____

If not, how can I correct the problem? _____

_____

_____

_____

_____

_____

Even if I have stayed on track, what loose ends, if any, still need to be tied together at this point?_____

_____

_____

_____

Once my loose ends are tied together, how do I utilize my caboose to re-emphasize the track, or one-sentence foundation, of my manuscript on which this train has been built so my readers will be more likely to take that foundation away with them? _____

_____

_____

_____

_____

_____

When you have answered these questions it's time for you and your partner to go your separate ways and return to your typewriter or computer or word processor. The ending to your piece may take several rewrites and a lot of time to complete, but it is worth every bit of time and effort necessary to properly construct your caboose. You would be doing the passengers on your train a great injustice if you gave them a smooth, enjoyable ride right up until the end and then shortchanged them on the caboose. In fact, you may want to come up with more than one possible caboose and then get back with your partner when you're both done so you can review and critique your endings and decide on the best one.

And then you'll be finished, right? Well, not quite. But you will have passed that seemingly insurmountable hurdle of taking that masterpiece that's been burning in your heart and turning it into a good, strong first draft, which you can now begin to polish and edit and polish some more. And that's a great achievement! Did you know that the vast majority of unpublished manuscripts are unpublished because the authors never took the time to commit their work to paper? Those masterpieces are still buried inside, and that's a tragedy. Never again can that be said about your manuscript, however. You have now laid your track and constructed your train; your dream is well on the way to becoming a reality.

Now, of course, comes the next hurdle—finding a publisher. I would be lying if I told you this is the easy part, but I would also be lying if I told you it was impossible. The publishing options are out there, and they're waiting to be explored. If you were determined enough to get this far in learning and applying the train-of-thought writing method, then you're determined enough to see this project through to its completion.

I wish you all the best in this exciting endeavor, and I look forward to traveling with you on your published word journey in the near future. Meanwhile I'll be listening for the call as your train prepares to leave the station: *All aboard!*

***

If any of you who have journeyed with me through this book would like to contact me, I would love to hear from you. You can reach me at:

www.kathimacias.com